CANOEING AND HIKING WILD MUSKOKA

AN ECO-ADVENTURE GUIDE

HAP WILSON

The BOSTON
MILLS PRESS

A BOSTON MILLS PRESS BOOK

Published by Boston Mills Press, 2003
© Hap Wilson, 2003

Cataloguing in Publication Data
Wilson, Hap, 1951-
Canoeing and hiking wild Muskoka : an eco-adventure guide / Hap Wilson.

Includes bibliographical references.
ISBN 1-55046-339-X

1. Ecotourism–Ontario–Muskoka–Guidebooks.
2. Outdoor recreation–Ontario–Muskoka–Guidebooks.
3. Ecotourism–Ontario–Muskoka–Maps.
4. Outdoor recreation–Ontario–Muskoka–Maps.
5. Muskoka (Ont.)–Guidebooks.
I. Title.

GV776.15.M8W54 2003   917.13'16044   C2002-901683-5

Published by BOSTON MILLS PRESS
132 Main Street,
Erin, Ontario N0B 1T0
Tel 519-833-2407
Fax 519-833-2195
books@bostonmillspress.com
www.bostonmillspress.com

IN CANADA:
Distributed by Firefly Books Ltd.
3680 Victoria Park Avenue
Willowdale, Ontario M2H 3K1

IN THE UNITED STATES:
Distributed by Firefly Books (U.S.) Inc.
P.O. Box 1338, Ellicott Station
Buffalo, New York 14205

Design: PageWave Graphics
Printed in Canada by Friesen Printers, Altona, Manitoba
07 06 05 04 03 1 2 3 4 5

The publisher acknowledges the financial support of the
Government of Canada through the Book Publishing Industry
Development Program (BPIDP) for its publishing efforts.

DISCLAIMER

The author, publishers and sponsors of this book shall not be responsible for any misadventures, misguided expeditions, property damage, injury or loss of life while using or relying on the information in this publication. *Canoeing and Hiking Wild Muskoka* is intended as a general guide only. It is not a substitute for proper research, skills training, physical conditioning, trip planning, scouting or other safety measures. It is the sole responsibility of the reader to determine whether or not he/she is qualified and capable enough to (i) safely participate in any activity to which this guide may relate; (ii) to undertake any fast or open water situations, trails, road conditions or other conditions; and (iii) to accurately assess conditions at time of travel.

Readers or users take full and sole responsibility for their actions at all times. Without limiting the generality of the foregoing, WHITEWATER PADDLERS are advised as follows: before choosing to run any rapid you must first evaluate for yourself; check water volume, water and air temperature, personal skills, fatigue, amount of freeboard, value and waterproofness of load, isolation, feasibility of rescue, availability of basic equipment and rescue equipment, and risk to your equipment and person(s). It must be understood fully that conditions change drastically with water levels and that detailed maps depict *average* conditions only, unless otherwise indicated. Personal flotation devices (PFDs) must be worn at all times. Safety equipment such as spare paddles, throw ropes and first-aid kits must be within reach. The use of helmets is strongly encouraged.

CONTENTS

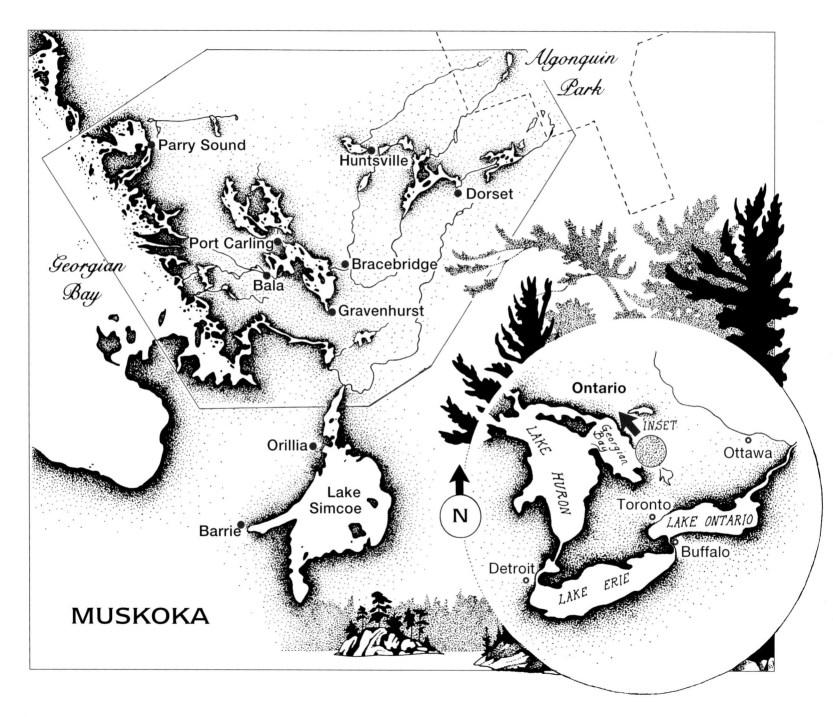

Parry Sound

Huntsville

Dorset

Algonquin Park

Port Carling

Bracebridge

Bala

Gravenhurst

Georgian Bay

Orillia

Lake Simcoe

Barrie

MUSKOKA

Ontario

Georgian Bay

INSET

LAKE HURON

Ottawa

N

Toronto

LAKE ONTARIO

Buffalo

Detroit

LAKE ERIE

FOREWORD

An idea, like a ghost, must be spoken to a little before it will explain itself.
CHARLES DICKENS

SHORTLY AFTER WE moved to a small farmhouse in Muskoka in 1996, my wife and I had a chance encounter with Bracebridge mayor Scott Northmore. Stephanie and I had just finished delivering some of our framed art to the Bird Mill Gallery, managed by Kim Northmore, and the three of us had decided to walk up the street to have lunch at Marty's Coffee House. "There's my father," Kim announced. "You have to meet him." The mayor peered up from his stranglehold on one of Marty's hefty sandwiches, and before introductions were even rounded out, I told Northmore that "Muskoka really needs an eco-adventure guidebook."

The mayor said nothing. He put down his sandwich, wiped his mouth with a napkin, stood up and walked to the back of the coffee house. "What did I say?" I asked Kim, who was as surprised as I was at her father's reaction. Great…. I've ticked off the mayor, I thought. Scott Northmore was talking into his cell phone, pacing the back hall, gesturing with his hand, and made occasional glances my way. After ten minutes he returned to our table, pushed the phone into my hand and said, "Talk to Murray. He'll set up a meeting." And

thus began this book, with the blessing of Muskoka Tourism.

Stephanie and I had only just started to explore the backcountry of Muskoka and we were beginning to realize two things. The first revelation was the existence of a unique system of waterways that, in general scope, remained undeveloped and surprisingly pristine; and second, that there was a paucity of field-friendly information accessible to the growing number of adventure tourists. Muskoka was typecast as a rather affluent cottage mecca, but what seemed to be inadequately represented was the rich and unique ecology of the region. Much of natural Muskoka was intact, but its charm was faltering in the wake of powerboats and jet-skis and the proliferation of golf courses and condo developments.

It took some considering to decide how to approach a project meant to protect threatened or disappearing wild and natural places for a region that, at first glance, seemed wholly developed and packaged as a cottage and resort playground. The term "wilderness" was hard to apply since most of Muskoka had, at one time or another, been logged over and trammelled by humans for the past two centuries. The hard nature of the Precambrian Shield landscape did, though, prevent much of the natural surroundings from being modified by development of a permanent nature. That was a good sign.

But an elite group of Muskoka "ghosts" quickly appeared at my door, each one demanding counsel. There were the representatives of human history to consider. Although Muskoka was used by First Nations people for hunting, fishing and seasonal gardening, it was not easily adapted for any perpetual habitation. And the histories of the exploration and exploits of the fur trade have little bearing on the historical cultural development and settlement of Muskoka. Tapping me on the shoulder with bony hands, though, were the *real* pioneers of Muskoka — the surveyors, the loggers, the homesteaders — each one adding to the delightfully explicit and provocative history of the Muskoka region. And as I continued to research the backcountry haunts, and talked to many of the longtime residents, I understood that there did exist a noble and almost fundamentalist self-esteem among those whose roots were well anchored in Muskoka granite.

The last and most persistent spectre was my own hubris. After years of trekking across true Canadian wilderness I suddenly realized I had become a bit of an adventure snob. I had set my compass point for destinations north, and to me nothing below North Bay was worth considering. But having made Muskoka home and a birthplace for our two babies, and being enticed out on a few local rivers by resident paddlers, I found that my somewhat fixed headspace about destinations was changing. Soon enough, the geographic parameters of what I'd thought of as a limited wilderness destination expanded until it equalled the size of Algonquin Park — over 7,000 square kilometres!

The more I travelled and explored, the more I saw the real character of this place called Muskoka. There is something very special here, with unique attributes aside from the obvious cottage persona — a naturalness that lies hidden among the granite and gneissic folds, and in the rapids, beneath the towering hemlock and pine, sheltered among the coastal islands of the Bay, and within the deep shadows of the highland forests.

There was quiet drama everywhere and, surprisingly, hardly any sounds of motorboats or cars. And there were places to stargaze unspoiled by the glare of manufactured light. And flora and fauna to wonder at, paint, sketch, photograph. And adventure! There were places to rock climb, exciting rapids to challenge even the most adept paddler, and endless winter trails that beckoned both the novice and the seasoned winter camper.

So, in the end, all the ghosts and the wild places of Muskoka had their say. I hope that I have captured at least some of the true essence of the magic here with these maps and explorations. All who visit and live here should hope for a continued rejuvenation of the spirit of the place — it is a goal worth striving for.

HAP WILSON

CHAPTER ONE

Ecotourism & the Muskoka Spirit

Though we travel the world over to find the beautiful,
We must carry it with us or we find it not.

RALPH WALDO EMERSON

ECOTOURISM

THE TERM "ECOTOURISM" was first coined in 1983 by well-known Mexican conservationist and ecologist Hector Ceballos Lascurain, and was quickly adopted by conservationists and tour operators. The rather loose concept has been around long enough now to determine what ecotourism actually embraces, how it works and how it doesn't. It's a complex intellectual principle that attempts to characterize an activity, espouse a philosophy and support a working model of sustainable development.

The relevance of ecotourism rests upon three assumptions: first, that ecotourism can promote and finance conservation; second, ecotourism can promote and finance economic development; and finally, ecotourism without a structured management archetype can destroy the resource it seeks to protect.

However, one must be wary of those who use the terms associated with ecotourism. Slick marketing language found in many travel brochures often misleads the traveller, and the "product" may have little or nothing to do with either conservation or economic growth. These terms include "nature tourism," "adventure travel," "self-propelled recreation," and "cultural travel," all of which define one particular activity. The International Ecotourism Society, which plays a strong role within the UN, offers this hybrid definition of ecotourism:

> *Ecotourism is a form of tourism inspired primarily by the natural history of an area, including its indigenous cultures. The ecotourist visits relatively undeveloped areas in the spirit of appreciation, participation and sensitivity. The ecotourist practices a non-consumptive use of wildlife and natural resources and contributes to the visited area through labour or financial means aimed at directly benefiting the conservation of the site and the economic well-being of the local residents. The visit should strengthen the ecotourist's appreciation and dedication to conservation issues in general, and to the specific needs of the locale. Ecotourism also implies a managed approach by the host country or region which commits itself to establishing and maintaining the sites with the participation of local residents, marketing them appropriately, enforcing regulations, and using the proceeds of the enterprise to fund the area's land management as well as community development.*

However, it is too easy to stray from the basic principles of ecology-based travel. Except for the purpose of accessing a destination, ecotourism activity should be "non-mechanized," though some tourist operators will argue this point vehemently. There have been problems. Purists will argue that whale observation boats interfere with the mammal's normal activity; so too do the hordes of camera-wielding nature lovers being flown by helicopter to watch the birthing of seals on the ice floes off the Magdalen Islands, or chasing polar bears around with the aid of gigantic "tundra buggies." Seeking out nature in this manner, even in the guise of ecotourism, does not necessarily improve the well-being of the particular animal being pursued. One of the biggest problems comes from the disruption of remote or primitive cultures that have been wholly transformed to adapt to an influx of tourists — villages being moved, forests being cut down to provide wood for the campfires and cooking fires of eco-travellers, modernization and the introduction of technology. All these changes have irreversible effects on a specific culture. This is where nature and cultural tourism should remain separate from ecology-based tourism.

I have taken some liberties by including "adventure" as one of the prime components of the eco-experience. Certainly, extreme adventure, such as rock-climbing and whitewater sports, would not conform to the pure definition of ecotourism. That is not to say that a rock-climber or whitewaterist is unable to have an eco-moment while carrying out that activity. A line does have to be drawn somewhere. The best way to observe nature without disrupting it is to climb into a canoe, or hike, or ski and trek off into wild places, remembering always that you are only a visitor.

For Muskoka to successfully implement a sound ecotourism base, there needs to be an established criteria of management and sustainability. That means a concerted effort from all local administrators, a program of public awareness, and strong community support. My intention, in travelling several hundred kilometres throughout the Muskoka backcountry, was to formulate and document a blend of adventure experiences with an ecological or environmental foundation. Since many of these special natural areas are threatened in some way or another, either by development or through disregard, we hope that public attention will be drawn to specific problems, thus accentuating the need for action and reparation. I hope this book will help to dispel the Muskoka typecast "cottage country" stigma and rekindle a sense of interest and pride in the natural Muskoka. The integrity of the Muskoka eco-adventure can be one of the things that makes this region unique.

Ecology & Adventure: Not-So-Strange Bedpartners

The concept of "adventure" has been around for some time. Think of adventure and you picture an activity that is different, unusual and exciting. It may have the added intrigue of danger or risk involved. Usually defined as something physical, adventure can include the emotional or spiritual experience as well. Your adventure could be fairly benign, as a simple walk in the local woods on a starry night. Or it could be a dangerous trek up Mount Everest. Adventure, in all cases, takes on the notion that you are stepping outside of your normal, safe or even familiar boundaries, and will be enjoying a new experience.

The term "ecology" was first coined by Earnst Haeckel in 1866. It wasn't until the world environmental revolution of the 1970s that it became an understood or even recognized expression. Ecology refers to the study of the interrelationships between organisms and their exterior environment. It's also the study of flora and fauna in relation to each other and to their habitats. All life forms, including humankind, are intimately linked with their environment.

An awareness of and regard for ecology can only make your adventure more exciting and rewarding. There are "soft" eco-adventures combining easy daytrips with comfortable lodging, and "hard" eco-adventures where your own personal skills and endurance are put to the test, compromising creature comforts for a more primitive experience. Whatever you are looking for, it's all here in Muskoka.

THE MUSKOKA SPIRIT

A Canadian settler hates a tree, regards it as a natural enemy, as something to be destroyed, annihilated by all and any means. The pity I have for the trees in Canada, shows how far I am yet from being a true Canadian.

JAMESON, 1838, *WINTER STUDIES AND SUMMER RAMBLES IN CANADA*

IF EVER ANYTHING could be said to epitomize the character of the Muskoka landscape, it would be its innate ability to withstand and survive the ravages of development. Muskoka is an anomaly by having managed to retain its charm and much of its ecological dignity under the constant onslaught of human "progress."

Early settlers and lumbermen cared little about conservation ethics and viewed the forest either as a nemesis or an inexhaustible resource. It wasn't until the end of the 1800s that there came a rude awakening — a realization that the magnificent stands of pine, once numbering upwards of 400 trees to the single acre, were now gone. Across the border, in 1891, the formation of the U.S. Forest Reserve Act was an admission that something had to be done to conserve the remaining forestland. That sentiment, luckily, was also expressed in Canada as the last of the pine, Ontario's provincial tree, drifted down the turbid waters of the Muskoka River on its way to the Gravenhurst sawmill. Alex Kirkwood of the provincial Crown Lands Department, concerned about the destruction of the Muskoka headwaters region, persuaded the government to consider a proposal for a park, and in 1893,

Algonquin Provincial Park was established as Ontario's first park.

One of the persevering traits of Muskoka is the historic use of the Canadian canoe as a means of travel and for recreation. The Huron people, master builders of the birchbark canoe, would hold "dream-guessing" feasts where the desires of the soul were revealed — canoes always ranked high as a primary material possession. Before the steamboat, pioneer road and rail era, the canoe was the only way to navigate the many lakes and rivers of Muskoka. Jimmy Bains and John Campbell, revered as Muskoka's first tourists, set up their permanent campsite on Chaplain's Island in Lake Joseph in 1866 under the guise of the "Muskoka Club," and were likely responsible for providing the initiative that jump-started the tourist boom.

The founding that same year of the Royal Canoe Club in London, England, by John MacGregor, who had just completed a trans-Europe trek in his wooden "Rob Roy" canoe, may have given sport canoeing its inauguration as a recreational activity across the British Empire. Recreational canoeing soon flourished in New England, and by the 1880s canoeing was one of America's favourite leisure activities. At this time too, Henry Rushton and E. M. White began producing the versatile cedar-canvas canoe that would revolutionize expedition canoeing in the Canadian North. Stories of canoe adventures dominated outdoor periodicals and books.

James Dickson, in his book *Camp Life in Northern Ontario*, described a canoe trip on the Muskoka River in 1886. "As we are now about to enter a section of country which is the undisturbed home of the deer and moose, of the beaver and muskrat, the man of the party who is the best shot and has the quickest eye is selected for the bowman of the foremost canoe. The loaded rifle, or double barrel, one barrel loaded with ball, the other with No. 3 shot, is laid carefully, the butt between his knees and muzzle projecting upwards over the bow of the canoe, ready to be snatched up and fired at any moment."

Recreational canoeing had yet to take on a more spiritual relationship with nature. The "great outdoors" was primarily a man's world, and the guided canoe trip through the Muskoka wilds afforded young men the experience to "build character" — and quick access to fish and game for the enthusiastic hunter.

But it was Tekahionwake, Pauline Johnson, herself a competent paddler, who immortalized the Muskoka spirit in her poetry.

Lichens of green and grey on every side;
And green and grey the rocks beneath our feet;
Above our heads the canvas stretching wide;
And over all, enchantment rare and sweet.

By the time World War I broke out in Europe, there were 46 established resorts operating in the Muskoka district. Cottages began dotting the shorelines as roads improved, and youth camps flourished, selling the "wilderness experience." Muskoka soon took on a more sophisticated visage, transforming itself for the urban cottager and transient resort vacationer; golf courses and marinas were built to fulfill the recreation needs of the affluent Muskoka cottager. The wilderness seekers began to deploy their canoes further afield, north to Temagami and east to Quebec. The Muskoka backcountry was abandoned and almost entirely forgotten.

If it weren't for the Muskoka Heritage Foundation, Muskoka Arts and Crafts Organization, the Field Naturalists and Camera Club, and a handful of individuals endeavouring to maintain the natural spirit of Muskoka, through publications and the visual arts, the mystique and magic that once defined Muskoka might have vanished completely. However, there still seems to be some complacency about ecological propriety. The expedience with which some decisions have been made — the cutting of 300-year-old pine to build tennis courts, or the construction of a snowmobiling bridge over McCrae Falls, for example — counters other positive moves towards sustained cultural stewardship and appreciation of the natural world. Many Muskokans would agree. The drift away from the natural world is, in part, an evolution of changing ideals and priorities, one quite often manipulated by planners and developers. It also means an absence of some of the things that best feed the soul — like clean water, pure air and a healthy environment. The Muskoka spirit is still alive, quiescent, waiting perhaps for our next move. It is my hope that the enchantment Pauline Johnson found so "rare and sweet" will continue to stir the hearts of us all.

MUSKOKA IN A NUTSHELL

There are numerous excellent histories about Muskoka; this is an overview of some of the defining features.

Physical Setting The landscape of Muskoka is chiefly a reflection of the erosional history of the southern Precambrian Shield. One-and-a-half-billion-year-old gneissic rock rises slowly as a peneplain, eastward from Georgian Bay (177 m above sea level), to the Algonquin Dome (over 500 m above sea level). The geological structure of folds and faults have created the unique alignment of rivers and lakes, while more recently, the Muskoka landscape has been heavily influenced by the retreat of the last glacial ice sheet approximately 11,000 years ago. Glacial Lake Algonquin covered much of Muskoka, its deeply silted shoreline marked almost precisely by the Highway 11 corridor. Glacial discharge left immense sand deposits along the Big East, Muskoka and Black Rivers. The movement of glaciers scarred and gouged the land, leaving Muskoka with either thin, acidic soil or no soil at all except barren rock ridges supporting sparse if any vegetation, especially along the Georgian Bay coast. This process of erosion and terrestrial shape-shifting has endowed Muskoka with dramatic landscapes and exciting waterways.

Climate and Hydrology Muskoka has a moist continental climate affected by prevailing winds off Georgian Bay. Coastal summers are about two weeks longer than those of the Algonquin Dome highlands further inland. The slope of the land results in a generally cooler climate and lower precipitation rate as one travels east. Lakes and wetlands are connected by a meandering network of creeks and rivers. The Muskoka River, the largest, is fed from the highland lakes of Algonquin by way of the Big East, Oxtongue and Hollow Rivers. At Bala, the Muskoka flow splits into the Moon and Musquash and finishes its westerly course through the bare rock ridges of the coastal plain and empties into Georgian Bay. A portion of the southeastern Muskoka district drains into the Black River watershed, which joins the Severn River, together forming the southern boundary of the region. Only the Seguin River lies outside of the Muskoka watershed, drawing its flow off the height of land along the northern Muskoka periphery.

Vegetation and Wildlife Forest growth varies, from the Eastern Upland deciduous region, dominated by sugar maple, beech, yellow birch, ash and red oak. Successional stands of white pine have a strong presence along bedrock ridges throughout Muskoka. Annual herbs include trout lily, fringed polygala, trilliums and numerous ferns. The semi-open, savannah-like character of Muskoka, most notable as one travels towards the coast, a mixed open forest of pine, red oak, juniper, black cherry and staghorn sumac dominate the forest scene with a sometimes scabrous understorey of blueberry, fly honeysuckle and wood fern. Muskoka has a proliferation of marsh communities, including conifer swamps of black spruce and balsam fir. One of the most dominant tree species, sought after for its bark used in the tanning industry, is the hemlock, found in all areas generally east of Lake Muskoka.

Because Muskoka is an area of ecological transition, it supports a diverse array of wildlife, including over 174 species of nesting birds, 54 mammals, 36 reptiles and amphibians, 70 butterflies, and 89 dragonflies and damselflies. Muskoka is the northern limit of the eastern fox snake, black-crowned night heron, yellow-throated vireo and willow flycatcher. Roaming their southern range you'll find black bear, moose, fisher and lynx, while bird species include the whiskey jack (Canada Jay), raven, spruce grouse, black-backed woodpecker and Cape May warbler. The red-shouldered hawk — a nationally rare species — makes its home within the hardwood forests of Muskoka. Along the coast one would see cormorants, osprey, terns, prairie warblers and, if lucky, catch a glimpse of the rare five-lined skink.

Land and Occupation The activity of the First People in Muskoka was sporadic and seasonal. Primarily hunter-gatherer in nature, they came to Muskoka to fish and hunt, for themselves and for trade. The resident Huron Nation was almost entirely wiped out by war and epidemic that raged through central Ontario in the mid-1600s. The British-backed New York Iroquois Confederacy abandoned Muskoka in the early 1800s, except for the Wahta Mohawks of the Gibson Lake area. The Ojibwa moved in and settled along the Georgian Bay coast and Lake Simcoe domain. Best known of the Chippewa of Lake Simcoe and Huron were Chief Mesquakie, also known as Yellowhead, from whose name came Muskoka, and Chief Aisance, who settled his band along the lee side of Beausoleil Island in 1842. Mesquakie, based out of the Rama area of Lake Simcoe in the 1830s, made regular forays into the heart of the game-rich Muskoka hinterland. Through various treaties, most of the prime Muskokan territory was appropriated from the Chippewa for a stipend allowance, although Mesquakie refused to sign any agreement with the whites. Yellowhead's lands to the north were subsequently sold off by Chief Mekis of the Muskoka Ojibwa, who made their territorial home at present-day Port Carling.

ECOLOGICAL BREAKTHROUGH

In 1987 the Muskoka Heritage Foundation was formed by a group of concerned citizens who recognized the need to protect Muskoka's built, cultural and natural heritage. It was a monumental step in providing a working group that would act as steward for the Muskoka legacy. Much of the background information obtained for this book was made available through the efforts of the MHF. They were instrumental in supporting a detailed documentation of Natural Heritage Sites in 1993–94, prepared by Ron Reid and Bonnie Mergsma, with the additional support of the District Municipality of Muskoka. Many of these sites have since been designated provincially protected areas.

How to Use This Book

ABOUT THE MAPS

All the maps in this book have been hand-drawn using the national 1:50,000 scale topographical maps as a base.

This is primarily a guide to the many water routes of Muskoka and in no way represents a full inventory of what is available to the naturalist or adventurer. Time and space considered, it features more of an author's selection. The actual region defining Muskoka, in the context of this book, deviates from the known or recognized political boundaries; rivers and waterways rarely obey the parameters of jurisdictional restraint. In dimension, then, Muskoka eco-adventure country rivals the magnitude of Algonquin Park, with two added features — an incredibly diverse coastal environment for kayak touring and general ease of access to all of the routes illustrated.

Although these maps are accurately drawn and detailed from field assessments, I still encourage travellers to use the standard 1:50,000 topographical maps as indicated for each route. Rivers are shown in bird's-eye view, while the more difficult or confusing sections, including rapids, are detailed in box insets. Specific rapid diagrams are not intended to make the running of whitewater easier for the inexperienced paddler. It is important to remember that navigable channels may vary with water levels. Many of the Muskoka waterways are under the influence of control dams; when open during spring run-off or periods of heavy rain, river navigation can be hazardous, especially for the neophyte. It is suggested that the traveller read some of the other available resource material listed at the back of this book to optimize the information on the route maps.

GENERAL MAP DETAILS	
Access/take-out point	Ⓐ
Viewpoint	Ⓥ
Portage in metres	
Rapids or swifts (Class I-II)	
Technical rapids (above Class II)	
Falls & dangerous chutes	
Prevailing summer wind/wave warning	
Roads	⑪
Bed & breakfast/small inn	✳
Campsites (large, medium, small)	▲ ▲ △
Scale in kilometres (map border)	

RAPID DETAILS	
Running channel flow	
Deepwater V entry	
Standing waves	
Rapid classification	CI-CIII
Eddy pool	Ⓔ
Ledge/rock	

Stock Recreational Tandem Canoeing

Modified Whitewater Canoes (Solo or Tandem)

Kayak Touring (Solo or Tandem)

Whitewater Kayaking

Wildlife Observation

Hiking

Cross-Country Skiing

GENERAL NOTE ABOUT ADVENTURE ACTIVITIES

Although this book is mostly meant to feed those aqueous passions for paddle and portage, I have included places to hike and ski and generally browse at leisure, taking in the sights and sounds of wild Muskoka. As with any outdoor activity, there exist inherent risks. But without some uncertainty and danger, life would be quite prosaic. Hiking and nature observation, on their own, pose little threat to life and limb, barring any sudden urge to free-climb a precipitous rock face in bare feet. Water sports, on the other hand, require at least a basic understanding of the skills required for personal safety. Whitewater paddling and open water kayaking can be dangerous fun. Even though many of the river routes in this book require whitewater skills, I have indicated which sections are applicable to beginner or novice paddlers, and almost every river has a length of its course devoted to that level of expertise. Please read over the following section carefully; it will help you decide which route conforms to your own level of skill.

WATER LEVELS & HYDROLOGY PATTERNS

It is almost impossible to make a perfectly accurate, average assessment of any river. The best we can do is to make the variables known to the paddler. Forewarned is forearmed. The travellers' ability to adjust to environmental change, including adapting to fluctuating water levels, is part of the overall skill of the paddler in making responsible and safe judgment calls. The information gathered in these pages regarding water levels has been based upon the "average" to lower water level conditions that prevail through late June to early September — when channels are clearly defined. This time period is considered the "normal" canoeing season. Discrepancies are noted where applicable.

High Water Conditions

Extreme high water conditions are not only very dangerous, but render some of the detailed rapid charts in this book valueless, except possibly noting the spring-level portage landings above dangerous water, which are quite often different from normal summer take-out points. Most rapids become unrecognizable, voluminous, often with flooded portage landings and very strong current throughout. In Muskoka, many spring runs can be executed as early as mid-March, even when headwater or lower basin lakes may still be impeded with ice. *These trips are not suited for novices!* Advantages to high-water levels include smoother ledges, submerged rock-gardens, exciting deep-water wave action and straight running channels. Concentration is focused less on spontaneous technical moves and more on keeping water out of the canoe. Obvious problems or risks may involve longer rescue time because of strong current, cold-water danger, submarining in big waves, and the added danger of hitting "snags" (fallen timber — also called "sweepers"). Since many of the Muskoka rivers are dam-controlled, it is best to check with the local Ministry of Natural Resources office for current conditions.

Low Water Conditions

Water levels that are lower than those described in this book may necessitate more lining, wading or portaging. Rock gardens, typically characteristic of all Canadian Shield rivers, may become rockier, actually constricting main channels (for example, the Moon River), while ledges become pronounced as actual drop-offs. Obstacles or obstructions generally become more visible and main channels more defined. The potential for getting hung up or broaching on "pillow rocks" is fairly high if you don't employ good technique. Because water volume is lower, you have more adjustment time while manoeuvring. Ferries and eddy turns have to be executed with diligence. Low water conditions sometimes allow more playtime along rapids normally too difficult to run during high-flow periods. Those who possess good whitewater skills and creative technique also have the opportunity to shorten or eliminate some portages.

Rating River Difficulty & Skill Level

The difficulty of a river or route is determined by risk factor and overall stamina to complete the trip safely. Variables such as weather, wind and water levels are unpredictable and should be considered when choosing a route. For example, the time spent travelling against a strong headwind or navigating rapids during unusually high water levels may suddenly change the general classification of a route. Specific rating factors for these routes include the number and difficulty of technical rapids, gradient or elevation drop per kilometre, length and difficulty of portages and their degree of maintenance, and any unusual characteristics. Individual rapids are graded in accordance with the International River Grading System and apply to stock, recreational canoes only. Out of a total grading of six on the IRGS scale, only the first three grades apply to open boats, or those canoes that are not seriously modified for extreme whitewater sport.

Know Your Skill Level

A growing number of well-geared canoeists have trouble admitting that they are, in fact, novice paddlers, and quite often will attempt running a particular rapid or route far beyond their capability. The mounting number of derelict canoes that decorate rogue boulders on our northern rivers attest to this grim fact. People have perished on Muskokan rivers. *If you do not have the compulsory skills, do not whitewater paddle.* You should either sign up for a clinic or join a guided expedition where you can learn the basic strokes, after which you can assess your personal level of skill and apply it to a route of comparative grading. Being able to read whitewater is an acquired skill that takes years to develop.

Rapid Classification

This classification of rapids conforms to the International River Grading System (IGRS), which includes a total of six classifications. Since Class or Grade III rapids are considered the maximum safe rating for open, stock recreational canoes, not modified for whitewater, only the first three grades are listed. Each class is defined, including "technical" ratings. This information will enable you to assess your own skills and experience and apply them to the routes described in this book.

CI: Definite deep water, clear channel with well-defined downstream V, small regular waves to 1/3 metre. Beginner's level.

CII: Definite main channel with optional secondary channels visible in high water. Rock gardens, ledges present with standing waves to 2/3 metre. Technical moves such as eddy turns and ferrying are required. Intermediate level paddler.

CIII: Maximum for open canoes – spray deck optional for rockered whitewater canoes but recommended for low-profile designs. Definite main channel with high volume, often narrow, steep-pitched V ending in an hydraulic/souse. Less reaction time. Boulder gardens, high ledges present with waves to one metre or more. Scouting and rescue spotters mandatory. Advanced level only.

CI — Easy (Low Risk)

CI tech.

CII — Moderately Difficult (Moderate Risk)

CII tech.

CIII — Difficult (High Risk)

CIII tech.

CI tech: As CI with greater volume or some minor technical maneuvers requiring basic skills. Advanced beginner's level.

CII tech: As above with greater volume and larger waves, rock gardens with indefinite main channel; may be clogged with sweepers, snags, logjams or larger boulders. Low-profile canoes may swamp. Experienced intermediate level paddler.

CIII tech or CIV: As above with greater volume, questionable main channels often split; tight passages and steep drops with serious aerated holes present. Specialized whitewater equipment/canoes required. Playboats with flotation or decked canoes only. Scouting and safety teams required. Expert level only.

SKILL CLASSIFICATIONS

The following skill level categories are predicated upon the paddlers' ability to safely handle a stock recreational open canoe. Each classification indicates the necessary skills required, route characteristics, and type of difficulty or hazard one may encounter.

Novice or Beginner

Skills Required Canoeists have little or no experience or knowledge of whitewater techniques but do have primary flat-water skills. Capable but not proficient at navigating easy Class I rapids or swifts only, while all technical rapids are avoided. May attempt next grade if accompanied by higher skilled paddler.

Route Characteristics Predominantly flat-water with some river or creek links that may have swifts or very minor rapids with the option to portage. Portages are not excessively difficult and water temperature exceeds 16 C (60 F) from June through August.

Hazards High wind on larger lakes and possible cold weather and water during buffer season paddling, or a sudden rise in water levels.

Experienced Novice

Skills Required Canoeists have basic whitewater skills and are proficient at safely navigating Class I and Class I technical rapids. Class II rapids and higher are portaged. Some basic lining skills (roping canoe on rapids); may attempt next grade if accompanied by higher skilled paddler.

Route Characteristics River gradient is generally consistent and gradual with sporadic drops exceeding 1.5 metres/kilometre. Predominantly Class I rapids interspersed with more technical rapids that can be portaged. Portages are generally easy, but with a few classic steep climbs, bogs, or long hauls (over 1 km). Water temperatures are above 16 C (60 F) during the summer months.

Hazards Same as novice with the addition of potential for capsize in easy grade rapids located above or close to dangerous chutes, falls or continued rapids.

Intermediate

Skills Required Canoeists are proficient whitewater paddlers and are able to safely navigate up to Class II technical rapids without difficulty. Class III rapids are carefully scrutinized and run only with safety and rescue precautions in place and/or accompanied by an advanced paddler. Eddy turns and cross-ferries are fully understood and implemented. Canoe extrication and rescue techniques are mandatory.

Route Characteristics River gradient is often steep-pitched with at least 50 percent Class II rapids or greater. Some longer Class I and II rapids may not have portages but lining is possible during lower water level conditions. Water temperatures may be lower than 16 C (60 F) during off-season paddling. Portages could be precipitous, longer than 2 km, and may be partially obstructed or overgrown. Environmental conditions are generally moderate.

Hazards Cold weather and water risk during buffer season trips, and the greater risk of capsize in larger rapids. Temptation to run the more difficult rapids is greater.

Advanced or Expert

Skills Required Canoeists have extensive whitewater experience and high-level skills. Ability to safely navigate Class III rapids or greater (with specialized gear). Paddling skills include all technical rescue and extrication procedures. High level of stamina and endurance under duress.

Route Characteristics River gradient has long, steep-pitched drops with a high proportion of technical rapids. Longer rapids may not have portages, and lining may not be possible. Water temperatures may be lower than 16 C (60 F) as with early "polar bear" runs during high flow periods. Portages extremely difficult or even nonexistent. Environmental conditions may be extreme.

Hazards Cold weather and water risk is much higher, as is the possibility of capsize in larger rapids in cold water. Wet- or dry-suits, added flotation to canoes, and spray covers are mandatory for high flow and cold-water navigation on long sets of rapids.

NATURE OBSERVATION

By plucking her petals, you do not gather the beauty of the flower.
RABINDRANATH TAGORE

Our appreciation and enjoyment of the outdoors is enhanced through knowledge of the environment and in firsthand experiences. Those who travel the river solely for the adrenaline charge of shooting whitewater often deprive themselves of other stimulating experiences that would otherwise enrich a holistic view of the surrounding ecology. Nature observation is more popular today than it has ever been; there exists a greater number of camera-toting, binocular-wielding field naturalists who prefer not to view wildlife through the sights of a gun. As urban creatures, we often distance ourselves from nature. We may even presume that wildlife is lined up along the shore waiting serenely for us to take photographs of them at our convenience.

Being knowledgeable about wildlife traits and habitat is essential for successful outings, whether you are interested in outdoor photography or simply in observing wildlife without disturbing it. Your method of approach, the wind direction, and seasonal variations — even the style in which you handle your canoe — can all affect what you will and will not see. The exhilaration of nature observation requires perseverance, patience, understanding and respect for the environment. Please do not harass wildlife, disturb nests, or pick or trample upon sensitive plants just for the sake of improving a camera shot.

A WORD ABOUT PRIVATE PROPERTY

Many of the recreational trails found within this book pass through or adjacent to privately owned land. Please respect this when looking for a campsite or portage trail. When in doubt, solicit the permission of the owner of the land you wish to cross through. Most Muskokans are quite obliging and helpful. Study your route and plan it according to daily distances to campsites.

THINGS TO BE WARY OF

Muskoka is a safe environment in which to travel but there are three life forms you should be aware of: the Eastern Massasauga rattlesnake, poison ivy and biting insects.

Rattlesnakes are uncommon and generally quite docile unless disturbed. They can be found along all coastal regions of Muskoka, more noticeably near Georgian Bay. You should familiarize yourself with the snake's characteristics and habitat, and dogs must be leashed at all times.

Leaves of three, let it be…. Good advice if you can't recognize what it looks like. If someone in your party is familiar with **poison ivy**, get them to point it out. Poison ivy grows sporadically throughout the district, especially at the perimeters of campsites and along portage trails.

Insects — those flying, buzzing, crawling, boring, chewing and biting vexations of the backwoods — are, without question, an integral part of the natural environment. Whether we like it or not, they assume their rightful place alongside us as we trek through the countryside. We are, after all, part of the cyclical food chain as soon as we step into the realm of nature. We may jockey for supremacy at the top but usually lose that declaration along with a good deal of self-control when it comes to putting up with bugs! I could write volumes about deterrents and fireside stories about biting insects, but in a nutshell, my best advice is to invest in a quality bug-jacket. Early May is peak blackfly season, while all other pests seem to disappear by late July. This coincides with some of the optimum spring photography and observation possibilities, and the best runs on most of the rivers.

Eastern Massasauga
Rattlesnake

Poison Ivy

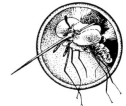

Insect Pests

Safety Precautions

On longer excursions, or those trips that assume a higher level of risk, it is recommended that someone in your party carry a cell phone. I've tested my own phone across the backcountry trails and found that only the stronger three-watt range "bag-phones" work outside of the Highway 69 and Highway 11 corridor (approximately 20 km distance). I've also used satellite phones that allow connection anywhere you go and are now affordable through purchase or rental. Know your route and all of the available evacuation points along the way in case an emergency arises.

Campsites, Accommodation & No-Trace Camping

On some Muskoka backcountry trails it may be difficult to find an established campsite. This is why it is crucial that you plan out your itinerary and be prepared to make adjustments according to their availability. Some routes lend themselves to more luxurious overnights, taking advantage of the many fabulous bed-and-breakfast establishments, camps and small inns along the way. See the B & B listing at pages 139–140 to find those who will accommodate the needs of the eco-traveller, through shuttles, bagged lunches, rentals and so forth.

No-trace camping is exactly what it sounds like — leaving no trace of your passing so that others may enjoy, so the peace and ecology remain undisturbed by your visit. It is our nature to create garbage, and our foible not knowing where to discard it. Muskoka rivers, vales, pine-topped ridges and fenlands provide us with the last remaining vestiges of wild landscape. Should we decide to desecrate it, then we will have no place left to enjoy that much-needed sense of connection with the Earth. We should do our utmost to protect what's left. All garbage should be taken out — and it wouldn't hurt the adventurer to clean up the trail as litter is found along the way. Until a regular maintenance program is initiated, all Muskoka backcountry trails are user-maintained. Keep campfires small, use established firepits, and use stoves whenever possible to conserve firewood. Some campsites have established latrines; if none exist, make sure you excavate a common toilet at least 30 to 50 m back from any body of water, trail or tenting area. Toilet paper can be burned in the fire, packed out or buried along with any human waste. Because soil is thin along the coastal regions, it is paramount that you find a suitable, ecologically sound location for your latrine, where soils are at least 20 centimetres deep.

Water Quality & Fish Consumption

Neil Hutchinson, water quality consultant for Muskoka, says, "I routinely drank water from the middle of Lake Muskoka while water sampling for the Ministry of the Environment." As a general rule, though, Hutchinson suggests that all travellers filter their water, especially any water taken near shore, where natural and human pathogens are a greater likelihood. Filtration removes particulate (silt and sediment) and sediment absorbs many water-borne pollutants. A good filter also removes bacteria and pathogens. Although Muskoka water appears to be crystal clear, don't take any chances — boil or filter all water used for drinking.

Hutchinson also adds that canoeists who like to fish should be aware of fish consumption guidelines. Fish are a far more efficient means of acquiring particular environmental contaminants — mercury being the biggest problem. Canoeists should refer to the Ministry of the Environment's "Guide to Angling" publication for the current year, generally available at beer stores. Both MNR and MOE caution women of childbearing age and children about the risk of ingesting mercury from game fish. Best advice is to limit your intake.

CHAPTER TWO

Muskoka Canoe & Kayak Adventures

Only by going alone in silence, without baggage,
can one truly get into the heart of the wilderness.
All other travel is mere dust and hotels and baggage and chatter.

JOHN MUIR

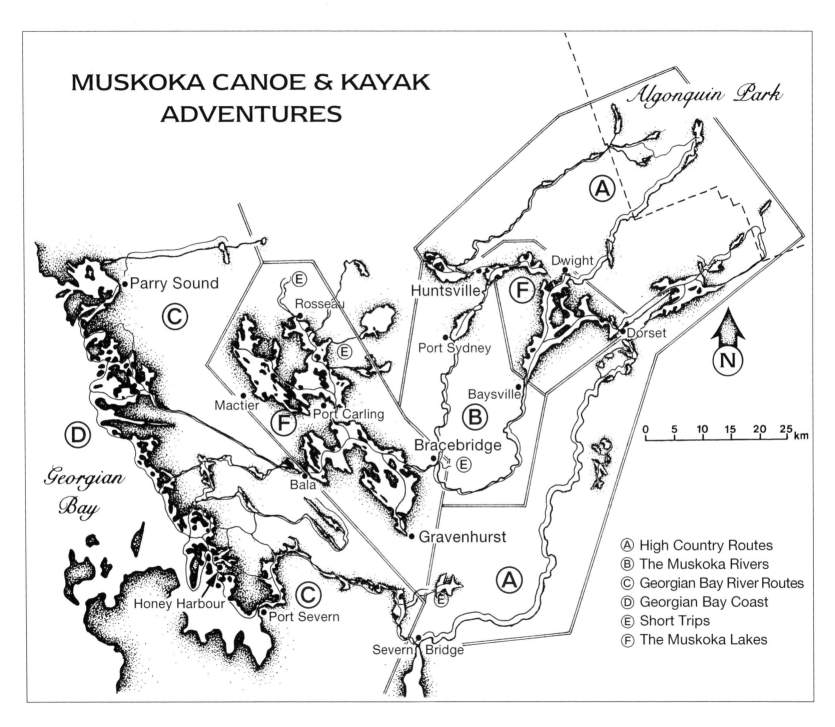

MUSKOKA CANOE & KAYAK ADVENTURES

Algonquin Park

Parry Sound

Rosseau

Huntsville

Dwight

Port Sydney

Dorset

N

Mactier

Baysville

Port Carling

Bracebridge

Georgian Bay

Bala

Gravenhurst

Honey Harbour

Port Severn

Severn Bridge

0 5 10 15 20 25 km

Ⓐ High Country Routes
Ⓑ The Muskoka Rivers
Ⓒ Georgian Bay River Routes
Ⓓ Georgian Bay Coast
Ⓔ Short Trips
Ⓕ The Muskoka Lakes

OVERVIEW OF ROUTES

A High Country Routes

Spilling off the "Algonquin Dome," these rivers run through a truly northern nature rich with wildlife. The granite and gneissic rock outcrops display the boldness of the Canadian Shield; the coarse-textured thin soils, swamp peat-lands and marshes support extensive flora, while adventure lurks behind every bend of the river or trail. The upper tracks will entice the ardent explorer while the gentler lower meanders will charm those who choose a more leisurely experience.

B The Muskoka Rivers

This is the heart of the Muskoka experience, defined by human and geological history, flowing dramatically through ancient glacial spillways into remnant pine forests and rocky chasms. Virtually intact, both rivers provide a full spectrum of eco-adventure possibilities, from exciting whitewater rapids and hiking to nature photography.

C Georgian Bay River Routes

Bold and reckless, these coastal threads carry a vibrant story of earth and human endurance. Beautiful beyond words, with a "rockland" persona, barren in places but not devoid of life, stark but stunning, sculpted by wind and time. Anyone travelling these soulful waterways will find both solace and inspiration.

D Georgian Bay Coast

Unique in many ways, including the greatest diversity of reptiles and amphibians in Ontario, this narrow coastal environment, with its windswept offshore islands, pine-capped shore ridges and hidden channels and bays, provides both adventure and escape for the touring kayaker or paddler.

E Short Trips

Chosen for distinctiveness and ecological personality, these specialty adventures can be explored in part or in their entirety, taking as little time as a couple of hours to a full, rich day. Make sure you take plenty of film — you'll explore some of Muskoka's seldom-seen waterfalls, and grand scenery is afforded to those who prefer to dip their paddles.

F The Muskoka Lakes

This quintessential bed-and-breakfast kayak adventure takes the explorer through a maze of waterways, past a unique architectural forum of development, among rocky, rolling pinelands and bedrock wetlands. This is one of the best introductions to this famous recreation mecca.

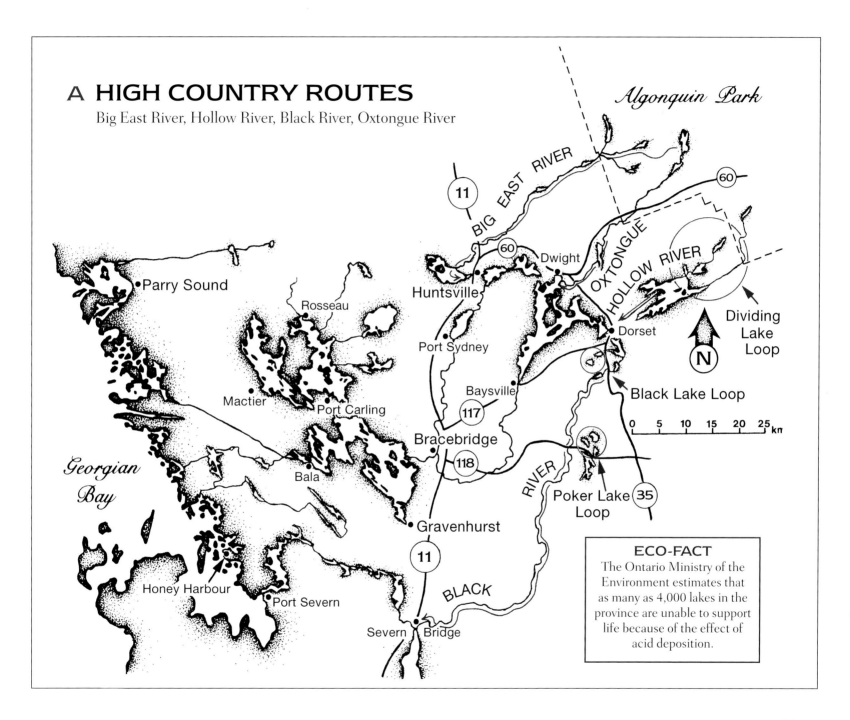

A HIGH COUNTRY ROUTES
Big East River, Hollow River, Black River, Oxtongue River

Algonquin Park

11

BIG EAST RIVER

60

60 Dwight

Huntsville

OXTONGUE

HOLLOW RIVER

Dividing
Lake
Loop

N

Parry Sound

Rosseau

Port Sydney

Dorset

Baysville

Mactier

Port Carling

117

Black Lake Loop

Bracebridge

*Georgian
Bay*

Bala

118

RIVER

Poker Lake
Loop

35

Gravenhurst

11

BLACK

Honey Harbour

Port Severn

Severn • Bridge

0 5 10 15 20 25 km

ECO-FACT
The Ontario Ministry of the
Environment estimates that
as many as 4,000 lakes in the
province are unable to support
life because of the effect of
acid deposition.

BIG EAST RIVER
Wabun noggin zibbi EAST SAND RIVER

The Big East is separated into three sections for easy reference: Ⓐ Canoe Lake to Distress Lake, Ⓑ Distress to Williamsport Road bridge, Ⓒ Williamsport Road bridge to Huntsville.

CLASSIFICATION Ⓐ difficult intermediate, Ⓑ intermediate, Ⓒ experienced novice

DISTANCE Ⓐ 34.6 km, Ⓑ 19 km, Ⓒ 34 km (22 km from Arrowhead/Highway 11 bridge)

TIME Ⓐ 2 to 3 days, Ⓑ 1 day, Ⓒ 2 separate sections or 2 days (or 1 very long day)

SEASON Ⓐ early May to June, Ⓑ mid-April through July, Ⓒ April to October

CHANGE IN ELEVATION Ⓐ rise of 30 m to Big East and 107 m drop to Ⓑ, Ⓑ drop of 46 m, Ⓒ drop of 13 m

PORTAGES Ⓐ 11 (6,830 m), can be reduced to 5,380 m; Ⓑ 3 (610 m); Ⓒ none

CAMPSITES Ⓐ 11 (mostly in park), Ⓑ 1 only, Ⓒ 3 commercial campgrounds

RAPIDS & FALLS Ⓐ 7.5 km runnable CI–CIII rapids, Ⓑ 7 (5 runnable CI–CIIs; some long), Ⓒ 1 easy CI

MAPS 31 E/6, 31 E/10, 31 E/7 (covers all three sections)

ACCESS Ⓐ Highway 60 to Canoe Lake, Ⓑ Highway 60 to County Road 8 to Billy Bear Road, Ⓒ Muskoka Road 3 to Williamsport Road bridge

TAKE-OUT Ⓐ Billy Bear Road bridge, Ⓑ Williamsport Road bridge, Ⓒ Huntsville town centre

FEES interior camping fee for one night in Algonquin Park

ADDITIONAL RESOURCE "Canoe Routes of Algonquin Park" map

SPECIALIZED GEAR Ⓐ wading boots, poling tip and old canoe (wetsuits for cold conditions)

WHITEWATER CHARACTERISTICS & GENERAL HAZARDS Ⓐ Very shallow conditions prevail after May, which means a lot of wading and lining along the upper course. During high water, some sections may hold particular dangers such as sweepers. Best running time is bug season — another consideration. Bouldery, shallow rapids require precise skills. Ⓑ Heavy spring volume and "ledge" drops require scouting and caution. Cold water hazard, and longer CIIs become extremely rock-choked in the summer. Ⓒ Navigable throughout season with one shallow riffle that may require wading after June.

ECOLOGY The high elevation and cooler climate supports a northern boreal ecology of white spruce, eastern white cedar, white and yellow birch and balsam fir. The upper river is one of the best environments to see larger mammals (moose, bear, wolf) in an undisturbed state. Below Williamsport Road the river passes through the steep, deltaic sand bluff shorelines of glacial Lake Algonquin, finally ending in a unique provincially significant wetland delta. The Big East corridor supports over 400 species of vascular plants and one of the most diverse collections of birds, mammals and herptofauna.

FEATURES When I questioned geographer-researcher Roger Bragg about the Big East headwaters, an uneasy look came over his face. "You've been there, then?" I asked. He said that he had, and that it was basically a "walking trip." That was quite some time ago, and although I knew that time hadn't changed things, I still had to explore it for myself. Well, Roger was partly right. I could see that one might experience some tough going in low water, but I loved it. It was hard work but worth the effort, bruised shins and bug bites and all. Few people pass through here, and *that's* a big plus. The mid-section of the Big East is a whitewater paradise. I've been on the spring run as early as April 9, when ice chunks still cling to the sides of the river. It's a full day of excitement and challenge for any whitewater enthusiast. The last segment is a naturalists' cakewalk, an easy cruise all the way to downtown Huntsville and a riverside cappuccino. There are many highlights: an undeveloped, natural environment, the Dyer memorial, unprecedented wildlife viewing, the Big East Delta and, of course, excellent whitewater excitement.

Big East River 1

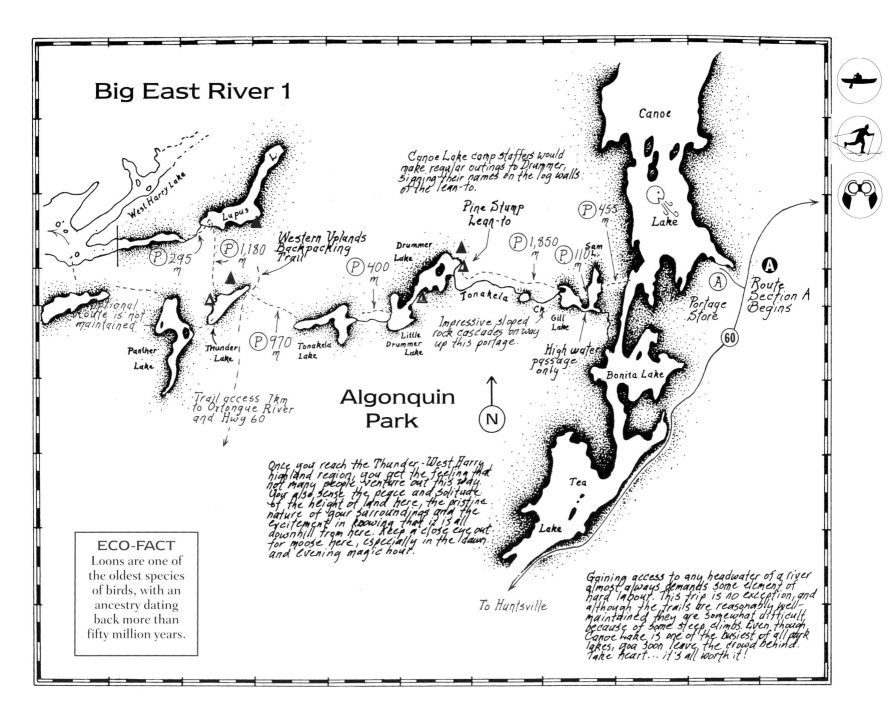

Canoe Lake camp staffers would make regular outings to Drummer, signing their names on the log walls of the lean-to.

Pine Stump Lean-to

West Harry Lake

Lupus L.

Ⓟ 295 m

Ⓟ 1,180 m

Western Uplands Backpacking Trail

Ⓟ 400 m

Drummer Lake

Ⓟ 1,850 m

Ⓟ 455 m

Canoe Lake

Ⓟ 1,100 m

Sam L.

Ⓐ

Route Section A Begins

Optional route is not maintained

Ⓟ 970 m

Thunder Lake

Tonakela Lake

Little Drummer Lake

Tonakela Cr.

Gill Lake

Portage Store

60

Panther Lake

Impressive sloped rock cascades on way up this portage.

High water passage only

Bonita Lake

Algonquin Park

N

Trail access 7km to Oxtongue River and Hwy 60

Once you reach the Thunder-West Harry highland region, you get the feeling that not many people venture out this way. You also sense the peace and solitude of the height of land here, the pristine nature of your surroundings and the excitement in knowing that it is all downhill from here. Keep a close eye out for moose here, especially in the dawn and evening magic hour.

Tea Lake

ECO-FACT
Loons are one of the oldest species of birds, with an ancestry dating back more than fifty million years.

To Huntsville

Gaining access to any headwater of a river almost always demands some element of hard labour. This trip is no exception, and although the trails are reasonably well-maintained they are somewhat difficult because of some steep climbs. Even though Canoe Lake is one of the busiest of all park lakes, you soon leave the crowd behind. Take heart... it's all worth it!

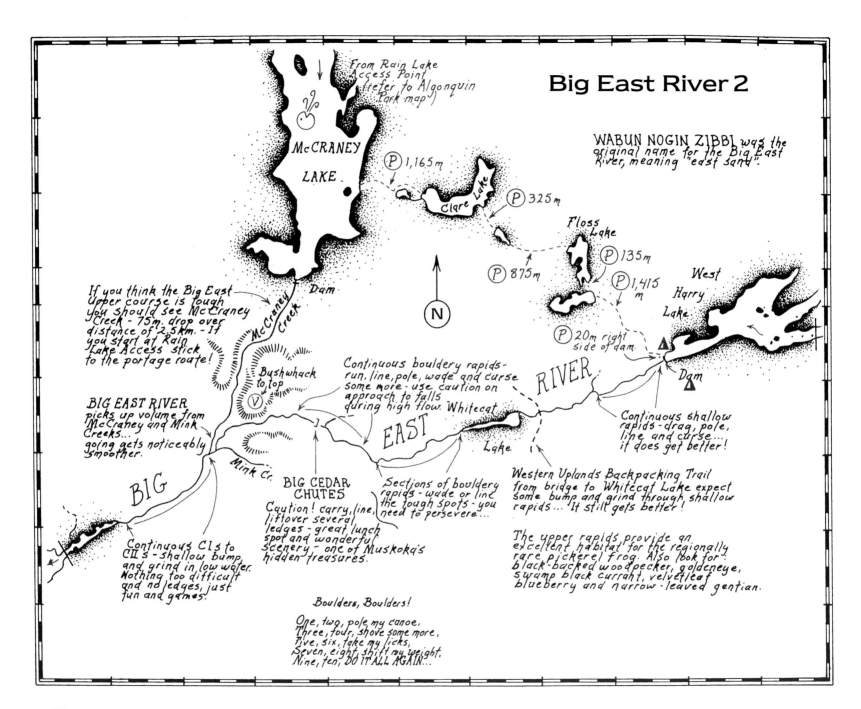

Big East River 2

From Rain Lake Access Point (refer to Algonquin Park map)

McCRANEY LAKE

P 1,165 m

Clare Lake

P 325 m

Floss Lake

P 135 m

P 875 m

P 1,415 m

West Harry Lake

WABUN NOGIN ZIBBI was the original name for the Big East River, meaning "east sand".

N

Dam

McCraney Creek

P 20m right side of dam

If you think the Big East Upper course is tough you should see McCraney Creek - 75m. drop over distance of 2.5 km. - If you start at Rain Lake Access stick to the portage route!

Bushwhack to top

V

Continuous bouldery rapids - run, line, pole, wade and curse some more - use caution on approach to falls during high flow. Whitecat

RIVER

Dam

Continuous shallow rapids - drag, pole, line and curse... it does get better!

BIG EAST RIVER picks up volume from McCraney and Mink Creeks... going gets noticeably smoother.

Mink Cr.

EAST

Lake

BIG CEDAR CHUTES

BIG

Caution! carry, line, liftover several ledges - great lunch spot and wonderful scenery - one of Muskoka's hidden treasures.

Sections of bouldery rapids - wade or line the tough spots - you need to persevere...

Continuous CIs to CIIs - shallow bump, and grind in low water. Nothing too difficult and no ledges, just fun and games.

Western Uplands Backpacking Trail from bridge to Whitecat Lake expect some bump and grind through shallow rapids... It still gets better!

The upper rapids provide an excellent habitat for the regionally rare pickerel frog. Also look for black-backed woodpecker, goldeneye, swamp black currant, velvetleaf blueberry and narrow-leaved gentian.

Boulders, Boulders!

One, two, pole my canoe,
Three, four, shove some more,
Five, six, take my licks,
Seven, eight, shift my weight,
Nine, ten, DO IT ALL AGAIN...

Big East River 3

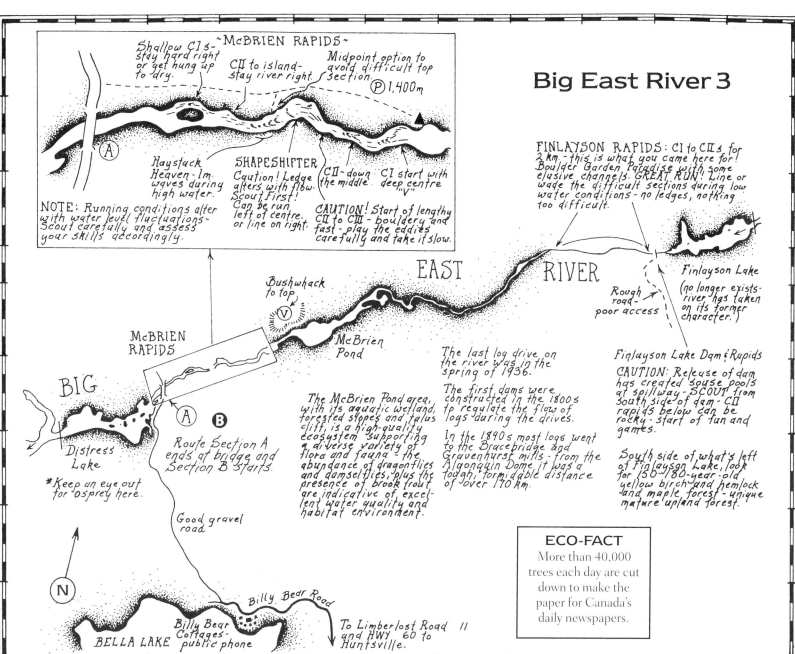

~McBRIEN RAPIDS~

Shallow CIs-
stay hard right
or get hung up
to dry.

CII to island-
stay river right.

Midpoint option to
avoid difficult top
section.
(P) 1,400 m

(A)

Haystack
Heaven - 1m.
waves during
high water.

SHAPESHIFTER
Caution! Ledge
alters with flow-
Scout First!
Can be run
left of centre.
or line on right.

CII - down
the middle

CI start with
deep centre
"V"

CAUTION! Start of lengthy
CII to CIII - bouldery and
fast - play the eddies
carefully and take it slow.

NOTE: Running conditions alter
with water level fluctuations-
Scout carefully and assess
your skills accordingly.

FINLAYSON RAPIDS: CI to CII s for
2 km. - this is what you came here for!
Boulder Garden Paradise with some
elusive channels. GREAT RUN! Line or
wade the difficult sections during low
water conditions - no ledges, nothing
too difficult.

EAST   RIVER

Bushwhack
to top
(V)

McBRIEN
RAPIDS

McBrien
Pond

Finlayson Lake
(no longer exists-
river has taken
on its former
character.)

Rough
road-
poor access

BIG

(A)
(B)

Route Section A
ends at bridge and
Section B starts.

Distress
Lake

*Keep an eye out
for osprey here.

The McBrien Pond area,
with its aquatic wetland,
forested slopes and talus
cliff, is a high-quality
ecosystem supporting
a diverse variety of
flora and fauna - the
abundance of dragonflies
and damselflies, plus the
presence of brook trout
are indicative of excel-
lent water quality and
habitat environment.

The last log drive on
the river was in the
spring of 1936.

The first dams were
constructed in the 1800s
to regulate the flow of
logs during the drives.

In the 1890s most logs went
to the Bracebridge and
Gravenhurst mills - from the
Algonquin Dome it was a
tough, formidable distance
of over 170 km.

Finlayson Lake Dam & Rapids

CAUTION: Release of dam
has created souse pools
at spillway - SCOUT from
south side of dam - CII
rapids below can be
rocky - start of fun and
games.

South side of what's left
of Finlayson Lake, look
for 150-180-year-old
yellow birch and hemlock
and maple forest - unique
mature upland forest.

Good gravel
road

(N)

Billy Bear Road

Billy Bear
Cottages-
public phone

BELLA LAKE

To Limberlost Road 11
and HWY 60 to
Huntsville.

ECO-FACT
More than 40,000
trees each day are cut
down to make the
paper for Canada's
daily newspapers.

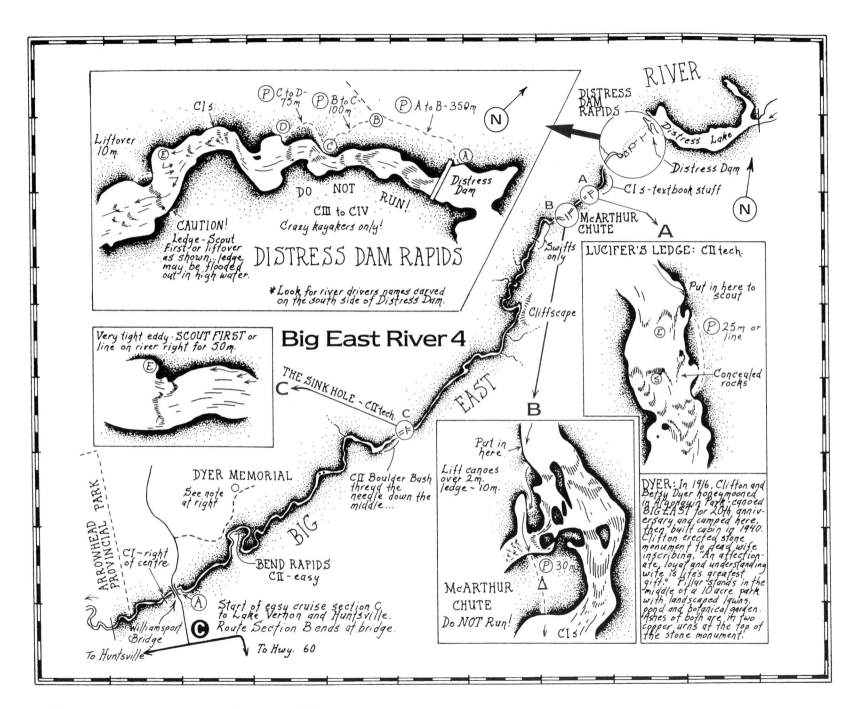

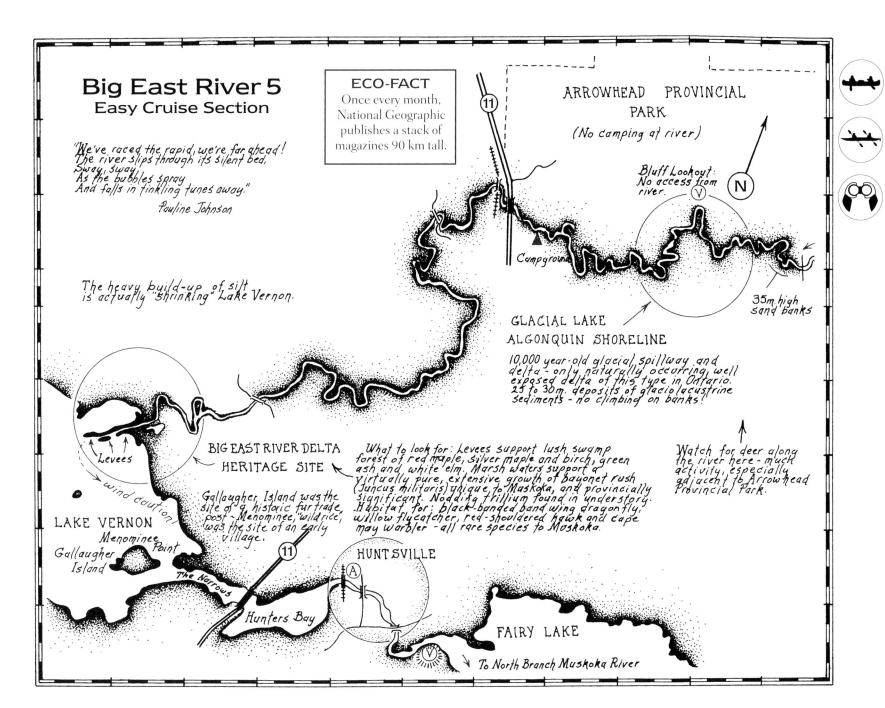

Big East River 5
Easy Cruise Section

"We've raced the rapid, we're far ahead!
The river slips through its silent bed,
Sway, sway
As the bubbles spray
And falls in tinkling tunes away."

Pauline Johnson

ECO-FACT
Once every month, National Geographic publishes a stack of magazines 90 km tall.

The heavy build-up of silt is actually "shrinking" Lake Vernon.

ARROWHEAD PROVINCIAL PARK

(No camping at river)

Bluff Lookout: No access from river.

Campground

N

35m high sand banks

GLACIAL LAKE ALGONQUIN SHORELINE

10,000 year-old glacial spillway and delta - only naturally occurring, well exposed delta of this type in Ontario. 25 to 30m. deposits of glaciolacustrine sediments - no climbing on banks!

BIG EAST RIVER DELTA HERITAGE SITE

Levees

wind caution!

Gallaugher Island was the site of a historic fur trade post - Menominee, "wild rice", was the site of an early village.

What to look for: Levees support lush swamp forest of red maple, silver maple and birch, green ash and white elm. Marsh waters support a virtually pure, extensive growth of bayonet rush (Juncus militaris) unique to Muskoka, and provincially significant. Nodding trillium found in understory. Habitat for: black-banded band wing dragonfly, willow flycatcher, red-shouldered hawk and cape may warbler - all rare species to Muskoka.

Watch for deer along the river here - much activity, especially adjacent to Arrowhead Provincial Park.

LAKE VERNON

Menominee Point

Gallaugher Island

The Narrows

HUNTSVILLE

A

11

Hunters Bay

FAIRY LAKE

To North Branch Muskoka River

HOLLOW RIVER

Kaweambejewagamog zibbi LAKE OF MANY HOLLOW SOUNDS RIVER

There are two sections to this route: **Ⓐ** the Lower Hollow River, and **Ⓑ** Dividing Lake.

(Note: Upper Hollow River not researched)

Ⓐ LOWER HOLLOW RIVER Kawagama Lake Dam to Dorset

CLASSIFICATION intermediate to advanced

DISTANCE 13.6 km

TIME 1 to 2 days (suggest one overnight)

SEASON late April through July (possibly longer, depending on summer rainfall)

ELEVATION DROP 40 m, or 3 m/km

CAMPSITES 3 small sites

RAPIDS & FALLS 17 (8 CIs, 7 CIIs, 1 CIII, 1 waterfall)

PORTAGES 2 (550 m) but can be shortened to 320 m

MAPS 31 E/7, 31 E/2 (includes **Ⓑ** route)

ACCESS Highway 35 to Kawagama Lake Road (1.6 km) to Maple Ridge Road (9.5 km) then to Dam Road (400 m)

TAKE-OUT Village of Dorset

SPECIALIZED GEAR Strictly ABS/Royalex riverboats or kayaks, wetsuits for spring runs

WHITEWATER CHARACTERISTICS & GENERAL HAZARDS Portages are user-maintained and, as with any Canadian Shield river, the rapids get quite "bony" during the summer. A look downstream from the Kawagama Dam doesn't necessarily give you a perspective of the flow, as the Hollow seems to pick up energy as you get further down, but at least you'll get an idea of whether or not you'll be walking the rapids by checking out the flow spilling through the gates. Canoeists must use extreme caution at Hollow Falls (also known as Hollow Chutes) — the last run starts off easy but gets progressively more difficult as you approach the falls.

ECOLOGY Because of the lack of development along the entire river, a natural corridor exists for wildlife and riverine flora. Look for the occasional moose feeding along the boggy shores in June. The water is remarkably clear, and as the waves in the rapids curl and thrash against the river boulders, the contrast of white against the grey blocks of granite accentuates the untameable beauty of the river.

FEATURES In 1874, James B. Shrigley built a saw- and gristmill at the mouth of the Hollow, 2 km east of Dorset. A dam was built across the river, flooding out a small riffle in order to raise the water level enough to drive the water wheel. Hollow Falls posed an obvious, huge problem for the log drives, so in the late 19th century, a 210 m log slide was constructed to bypass the impressive sloped-rock chasm. You can still see some of the remains of the logging works if you look carefully along the shore, opposite the portage. The Hollow is one of Muskoka's finest whitewater runs. It travels through pristine woods. Its drainage basin gathers water from the highlands of Algonquin Park, where the ridges rise to heights greater than 550 m above sea level — to the highest point in south-central Ontario. The clear water, emerald and pure, passes through rocky ridges and tumbles over cascading chutes and rapids to join with the general flow of the Muskoka waterway en route to Georgian Bay.

Ⓑ DIVIDING LAKE AND UPPER HOLLOW RIVER LOOP

CLASSIFICATION This is a 50 km, experienced novice loop that requires 3 to 4 days to complete. There are some long portages to contend with (totalling over 6.5 km), which may be a consideration for those who do not have lightweight Kevlar canoes.

FEATURES AND ECOLOGY The Reserve is a miniscule patch of pine, smaller than 137 ha, but it did protect and isolate centuries-old, giant white pine — a rarity in the province, which is ironic, since the white pine is Ontario's provincial tree! The Ontario government plans to further expand this special area to 7,289 ha, from Kawagama to Crossover and north to Ragged Lake. Because it is an "Enhanced Management Area," just about anything goes, depending on who makes the most noise. The hope is that canoeists using this loop will take a stand when pressure mounts to access this region by logging companies. Generally, the old pine is mixed with mature hardwoods (maple and beech) — it's good bear country, too — and some trees are in excess of 100 cm wide and 35 m high.

ROUTE OPTIONS To avoid low water levels on the Upper Hollow, paddlers can choose to make straight runs in either direction between the Livingston Lake access and the Snake Lake access in Algonquin Park. A car shuttle would be required.

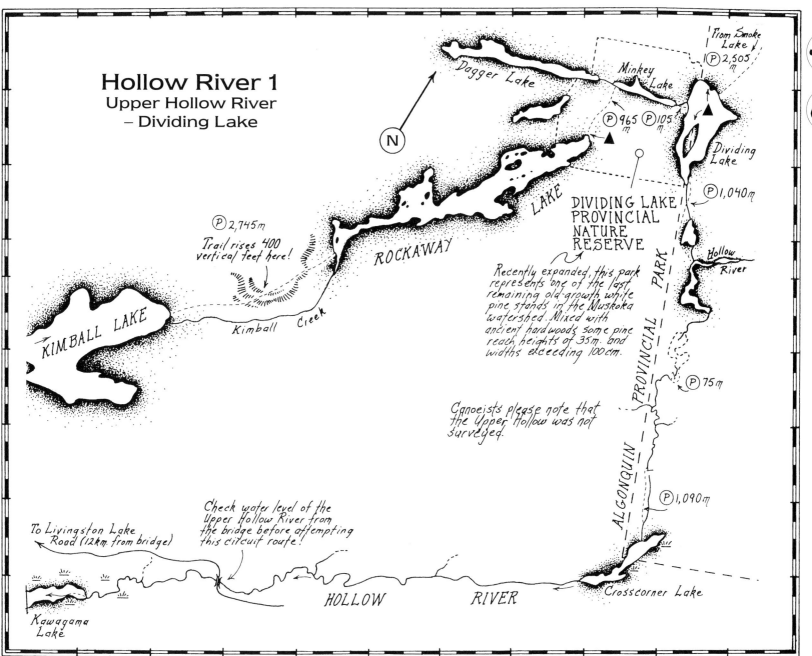

Hollow River 1
Upper Hollow River
– Dividing Lake

Dagger Lake

Minkey Lake

From Smoke Lake Ⓟ 2,505 m

Ⓝ

Ⓟ 965 m Ⓟ 105 m

Dividing Lake

Ⓟ 1,040 m

DIVIDING LAKE PROVINCIAL NATURE RESERVE

ROCKAWAY *LAKE*

Ⓟ 2,745 m

Trail rises 400 vertical feet here!

Hollow River

Recently expanded, this park represents one of the last remaining old-growth white pine stands in the Muskoka watershed. Mixed with ancient hardwoods some pine reach heights of 35 m. and widths exceeding 100 cm.

Ⓟ 75 m

KIMBALL LAKE

Kimball Creek

ALGONQUIN PROVINCIAL PARK

Canoeists please note that the Upper Hollow was not surveyed.

Ⓟ 1,090 m

Check water level of the Upper Hollow River from the bridge before attempting this circuit route!

To Livingston Lake Road (12 km. from bridge)

HOLLOW RIVER

Crosscorner Lake

Kawagama Lake

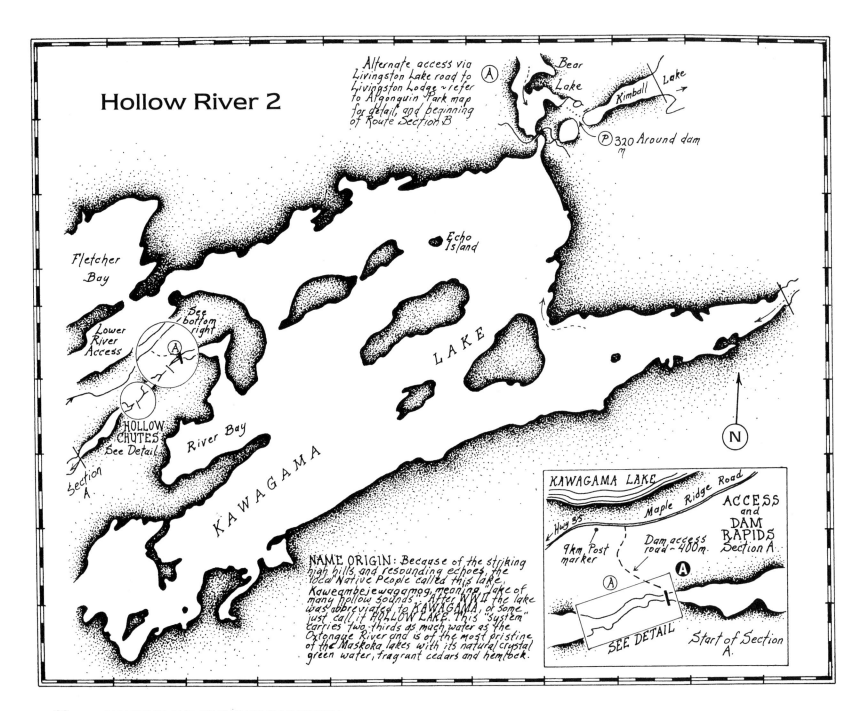

Hollow River 2

Alternate access via Livingston Lake road to Livingston Lodge ~ refer to Algonquin Park map for detail, and beginning of Route Section B

(A)

Bear Lake

Kimball Lake

(P) 320 Around dam
m

Fletcher Bay

Echo Island

LAKE

See bottom right

Lower River Access

(A)

N

HOLLOW CHUTES
See Detail

River Bay

KAWAGAMA

Section A.

KAWAGAMA

NAME ORIGIN: Because of the striking high hills and resounding echoes, the local Native People called this lake, Kaweambejewagamog, meaning "lake of many hollow sounds". After WWII the lake was abbreviated to KAWAGAMA, or some just call it HOLLOW LAKE. This "system" carries two-thirds as much water as the Oxtongue River and is of the most pristine of the Muskoka lakes with its natural crystal green water, fragrant cedars and hemlock.

KAWAGAMA LAKE

Maple Ridge Road

Hwy 35

ACCESS and DAM RAPIDS Section A

9km Post marker

Dam access road ~ 400m.

(A)

(A)

SEE DETAIL

Start of Section A.

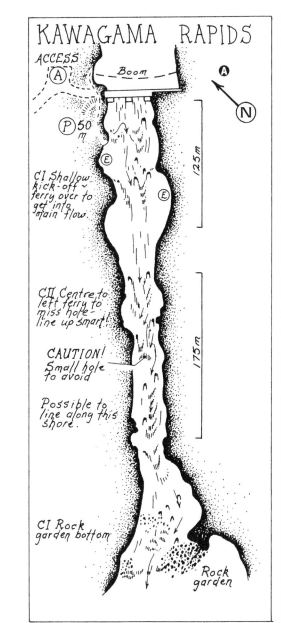

KAWAGAMA RAPIDS

ACCESS

(A)

Boom

(A) N

(P) 50 m

125m

(E)

CI Shallow
kick-off ~
ferry over to
get into
main flow.

(E)

175m

CII Centre to
left ferry to
miss hole ~
line up smart!

CAUTION!
Small hole
to avoid

Possible to
line along this
shore.

CI Rock
garden bottom

Rock
garden

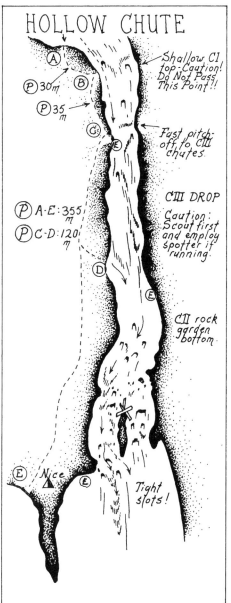

HOLLOW CHUTE

(A)

(P) 30 m
(B)

(P) 35 m

(C)

(E)

Shallow CI
top - Caution!
Do Not Pass
This Point!!

Fast pitch-
off to CIII
chutes.

CIII DROP

Caution:
Scout first
and employ
spotter if
running.

(P) A·E: 355 m

(P) C·D: 120 m

(D)

(E)

CII rock
garden
bottom

(E) Nice
△

(E)

Tight
slots!

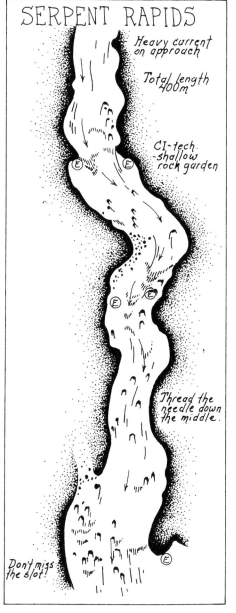

SERPENT RAPIDS

Heavy current
on approach

Total length
400m

CI-tech
shallow
rock garden

(E)
(E)

(E)
(E)

Thread the
needle down
the middle.

Don't miss
the slot!

(E)

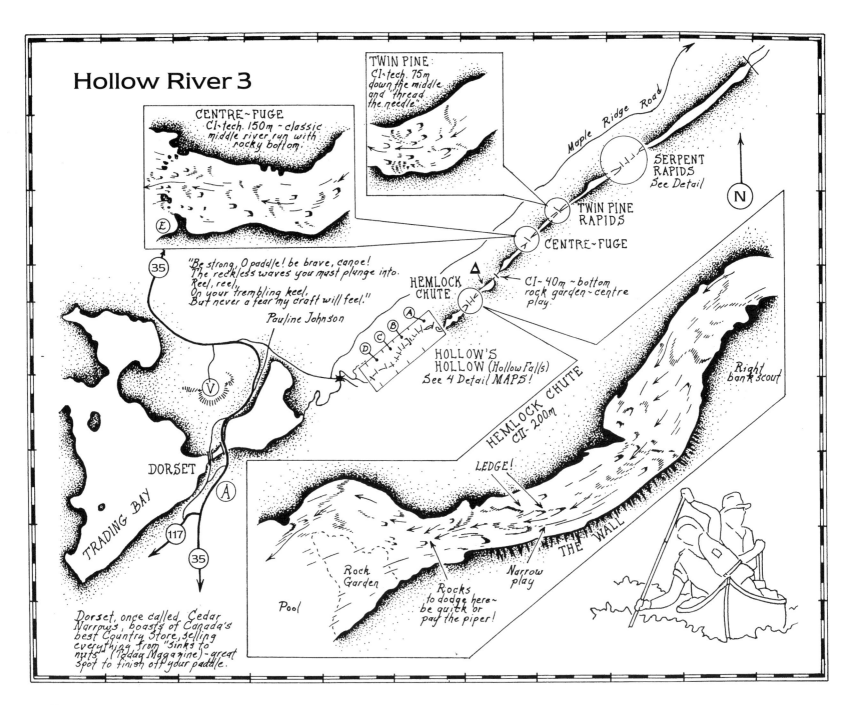

Hollow River 3

CENTRE~FUGE
CI·tech. 150m ~classic middle river run with rocky bottom.

Ⓔ

TWIN PINE:
CI·tech. 75m down the middle and "thread the needle"

Maple Ridge Road

SERPENT RAPIDS See Detail

Ⓝ

TWIN PINE RAPIDS

CENTRE~FUGE

Δ

CI~40m ~bottom rock garden~centre play

HEMLOCK CHUTE

③⑤

"Be strong, O paddle! be brave, canoe!
The reckless waves you must plunge into.
Reel, reel,
On your trembling keel,
But never a fear my craft will feel."

Pauline Johnson

Ⓐ
Ⓑ
Ⓒ
Ⓓ

HOLLOW'S HOLLOW (Hollow Falls) See 4 Detail MAPS!

Ⓥ

HEMLOCK CHUTE CII~200m

Right bank scout

LEDGE!

DORSET

Ⓐ

THE WALL

①①⑦

③⑤

TRADING BAY

Rock Garden

Narrow play

Pool

Rocks to dodge here~ be quick or pay the piper!

Dorset, once called Cedar Narrows, boasts of Canada's best Country Store, selling everything from "sinks to nuts" (Today Magazine) ~great spot to finish off your paddle.

Hollow's Hollow CII–CV 20 m drop over 1.5 km Classic Boulder Bash

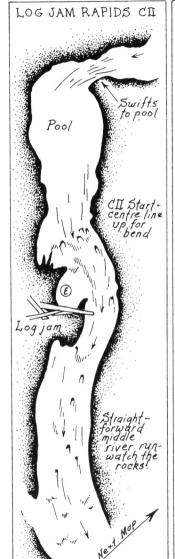

LOG JAM RAPIDS CII

Swifts to pool

Pool

CII Start-centre line up for bend

E

Log jam

Straight-forward middle river run-watch the rocks!

Next Map

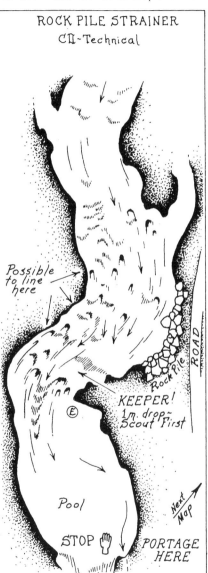

ROCK PILE STRAINER
CII-Technical

Possible to line here

ROAD

Rock Pile

E

KEEPER!
1 m. drop-Scout First

Pool

STOP 👆

Next Map

PORTAGE HERE

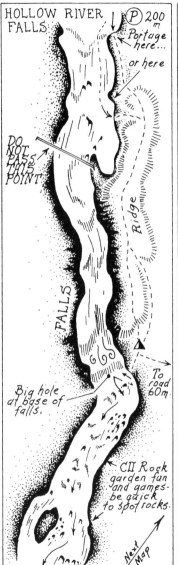

HOLLOW RIVER FALLS

P 200 m
Portage here... or here

DO NOT PASS THIS POINT

Ridge

FALLS

Big hole at base of falls.

To road 60 m

CII Rock garden fun and games-be quick to spot rocks.

Next Map

PIN BALL RAPIDS CII

Tight eddy

E

NOT FOR THE SQUEAMISH

E

CLASSIC BOULDER BASH

Swifts from here

BLACK RIVER
MUSKOKA'S GREATEST SECRET

The Black River is divided into three sections for easy reference: **A** Highway 35 to Highway 118, **B** Highway 118 to Victoria Falls, **C** Victoria Falls to Cooper's Falls.

CLASSIFICATION **A**, **B** and **C** are all experienced novice routes (all difficult rapids are portaged).
DISTANCE **A** 36 km, **B** 40 km, **C** 18 km
TIME **A** 2 days, **B** 2 days, **C** 1 day (2 days if paddling to Severn Bridge)
SEASON **A** break-up / mid-April to late May, **B** and **C** May to early October
ELEVATION DROP **A** 12 m, **B** 25 m, **C** 20 m
CAMPSITES **A** 5 sites, **B** 7 sites, **C** 3 sites
RAPIDS & FALLS **A** 6 runnable CIs, 4 waterfalls; **B** 10 runnable CIs–CIIs, 5 waterfalls; **C** 2 runnable rapids, 4 waterfalls.
PORTAGES **A** 6 (891 m); **B** 6 (800 m); **C** 4 (1,295 m), excludes portages around easier rapids)
MAPS all sections: 31 E/2, 31 E/3 (2 km section only), 31 D/14, 31 D/11
ACCESS **A** Highway 35 at signed parking lot at Little Wren Lake, **B** Highway 118 (no parking), **C** Cooper's Falls Road to Victoria Falls (rough dirt-pack, gravel road near end)
TAKE-OUT **A** Highway 118 bridge, **B** Victoria Falls, **C** Cooper's Falls
ADDITIONAL RESOURCES Kevin Callan's *A Paddler's Guide to Ontario's Cottage Country,* and Ron Reid and Janet Grand's *Paddling Ontario's Rivers*
SPECIALIZED GEAR wetsuits for spring runs and general touring/whitewater boats
WHITEWATER CHARACTERISTICS & GENERAL HAZARDS Take an old clunker boat down **A**; you'll be dragging it over deadfalls and gravel bars. The lower river can be run in playboats or touring canoes. The more difficult rapids are well illustrated — just be wary of the approach to any portage landing while paddling in high water flow.

ECOLOGY Ron Reid, co-author with Janet Grand of *Paddling Ontario's Rivers,* says of the Black: "The stained waters of the Black River seem to me to embody the essence of the endless forests of the Canadian Shield — dark and mysterious, slightly forbidding, and yet full of life and movement." The Black River landscape is personified by the banded gneissic ramparts — carved, scoured and smoothed by glaciers and time. The upper river is a wilderness paradise, albeit an undeveloped anomaly. There was so much deer and beaver activity, I was concerned that one or the other would have eventually leapt off the bank of the river and into my canoe! Most of the big pine is gone — logged out. There are, though, some gargantuan trees still living along the river in surprising numbers. The forest provides habitat for a diversity of shrubs and ferns, warblers, vireos and sparrows. Cardinal flowers bloom in late summer along the mud banks, adding a sudden blaze of red against the verdant backdrop of evergreens. Look carefully along the lower river for snapping turtles and the vivid blue tail of the five-lined skink — Ontario's only lizard — hiding under a log.
FEATURES The Black can be run in its entirety or broken into three sections, each course offering its own brand of adventure and scenery. It is steeped in history far too complex to cover here; to learn more, consult the additional resource books before heading out downriver.

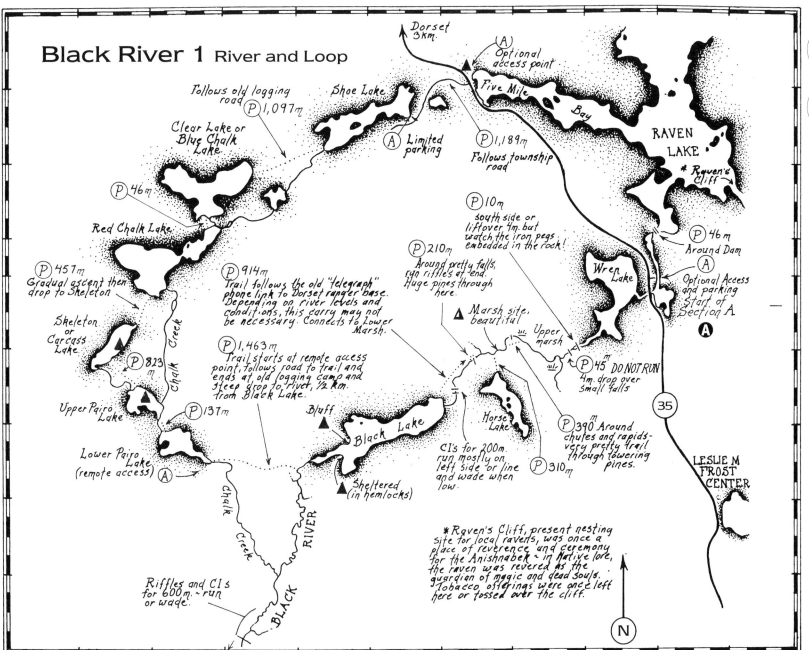

Black River 1 River and Loop

Dorset 3km.

Ⓐ Optional access point

Shoe Lake

Five Mile Bay

RAVEN LAKE

Follows old logging road Ⓟ 1,097m

Clear Lake or Blue Chalk Lake

Ⓐ Limited parking

Ⓟ 1,189m Follows township road

* Raven's Cliff

Ⓟ 46m

Ⓟ 46m Around Dam

Red Chalk Lake

Ⓟ 10m south side or liftover 4m. but watch the iron pegs embedded in the rock!

Ⓟ 210m Around pretty falls, run riffles at end. Huge pines through here.

Wren Lake

Ⓐ Optional Access and parking Start of Section A

Ⓟ 457m Gradual ascent then drop to Skeleton

Ⓟ 914m Trail follows the old "telegraph" phone link to Dorset ranger base. Depending on river levels and conditions, this carry may not be necessary. Connects to Lower Marsh.

△ Marsh site, beautiful

Upper marsh

Skeleton or Carcass Lake

Ⓟ 823m

Chalk Creek

Ⓟ 1,463m Trail starts at remote access point, follows road to trail and ends at old logging camp and steep drop to river, ½ km. from Black Lake.

Ⓟ 45m DO NOT RUN 4m. drop over small falls

Ⓐ

Upper Pairo Lake

△

Ⓟ 137m

Bluff △

Black Lake

Horse Lake

Ⓟ 390m Around chutes and rapids- very pretty trail through towering pines.

Lower Pairo Lake (remote access) Ⓐ

Ⓟ 310m

Chalk Creek

BLACK RIVER

△ Sheltered (in hemlocks)

CI's for 200m. run mostly on left side or line and wade when low.

35

LESLIE M FROST CENTER

Riffles and CI's for 600m. ~ run or wade.

* Raven's Cliff, present nesting site for local ravens, was once a place of reverence and ceremony for the Anishnabek ~ in Native lore, the raven was revered as the guardian of magic and dead souls. Tobacco offerings were once left here or tossed over the cliff.

Ⓝ

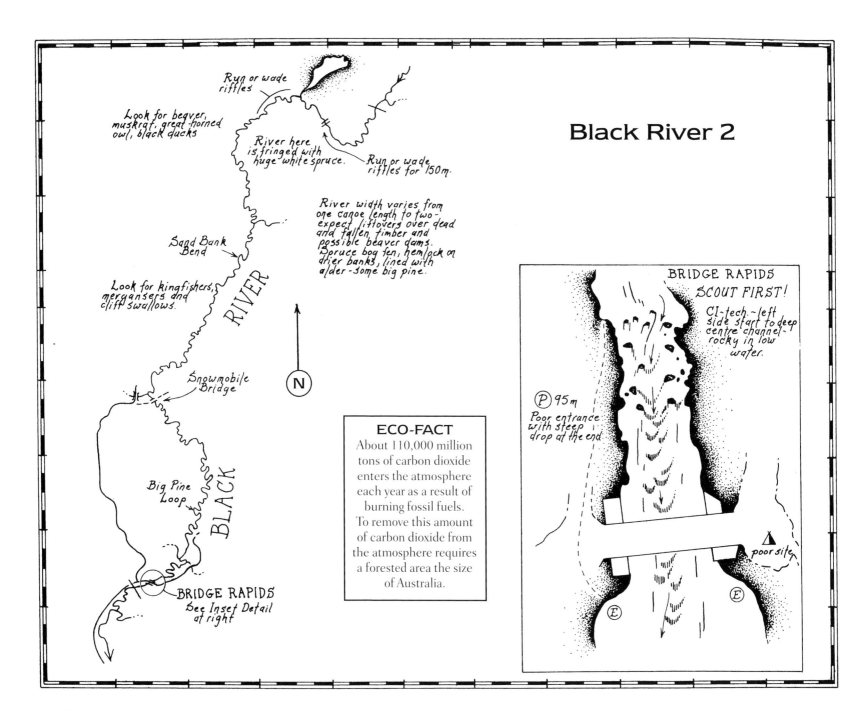

Black River 2

Run or wade riffles

Look for beaver, muskrat, great-horned owl, black ducks

River here is fringed with huge white spruce.

Run or wade riffles for 150m.

River width varies from one canoe length to two- expect liftovers over dead and fallen timber and possible beaver dams. Spruce bog fen, hemlock on drier banks, lined with alder - some big pine.

Sand Bank Bend

Look for kingfishers, mergansers and cliff swallows.

RIVER

N

Snowmobile Bridge

BLACK

Big Pine Loop

BRIDGE RAPIDS
See Inset Detail at right

ECO-FACT

About 110,000 million tons of carbon dioxide enters the atmosphere each year as a result of burning fossil fuels. To remove this amount of carbon dioxide from the atmosphere requires a forested area the size of Australia.

BRIDGE RAPIDS
SCOUT FIRST!
CI-tech.- left side start to deep centre channel- rocky in low water.

P 95m
Poor entrance with steep drop at the end

poor site

E   E

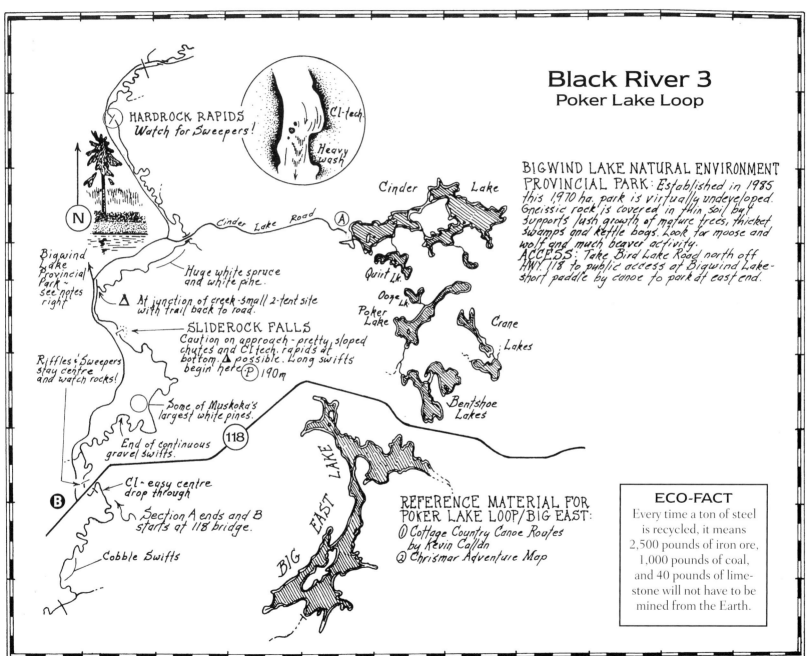

HARDROCK RAPIDS
Watch for Sweepers!

Cl-tech

Heavy wash

N

Bigwind Lake Provincial Park – see notes right

Cinder Lake Road

Ⓐ

Huge white spruce and white pine.

△ At junction of creek - small 2-tent site with trail back to road.

SLIDEROCK FALLS
Caution on approach - pretty sloped chutes and Cl tech. rapids at bottom. △ possible. Long swifts begin here. Ⓟ 190m

Riffles & Sweepers stay centre and watch rocks!

Some of Muskoka's largest white pines.

End of continuous gravel swifts.

⑴⑴⑧

Cl - easy centre drop through

Ⓑ

Section A ends and B starts at 118 bridge.

Cobble Swifts

Cinder Lake

Quirt Lk.

Ooze Lk.

Poker Lake

Crane Lakes

Bentshoe Lakes

BIG EAST LAKE

Black River 3
Poker Lake Loop

BIGWIND LAKE NATURAL ENVIRONMENT PROVINCIAL PARK: *Established in 1985 this 1,970 ha. park is virtually undeveloped. Gneissic rock is covered in thin soil but supports lush growth of mature trees, thicket swamps and kettle bogs. Look for moose and wolf and much beaver activity.*
ACCESS: *Take Bird Lake Road north off HWY. 118 to public access at Bigwind Lake - short paddle by canoe to park at east end.*

REFERENCE MATERIAL FOR POKER LAKE LOOP/BIG EAST:
① *Cottage Country Canoe Routes by Kevin Callan*
② *Chrismar Adventure Map*

ECO-FACT
Every time a ton of steel is recycled, it means 2,500 pounds of iron ore, 1,000 pounds of coal, and 40 pounds of limestone will not have to be mined from the Earth.

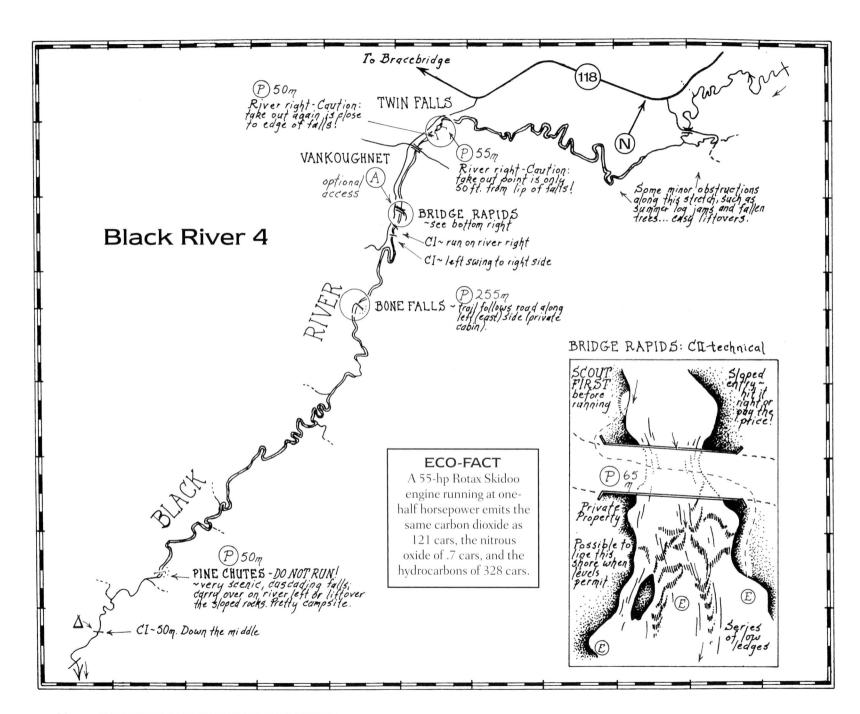

Black River 4

To Bracebridge

118

N

Ⓟ 50m
River right - Caution:
take out again is close
to edge of falls!

TWIN FALLS

Ⓟ 55m
River right - Caution:
take out point is only
50 ft. from lip of falls!

VANKOUGHNET

Some minor obstructions
along this stretch, such as
summer log jams and fallen
trees... easy liftovers.

optional
access

Ⓐ

BRIDGE RAPIDS
~see bottom right

CI~ run on river right

CI~ left swing to right side

RIVER

Ⓟ 255m
BONE FALLS ~ trail follows road along
left (east) side (private
cabin).

BRIDGE RAPIDS: CⅡ-technical

SCOUT
FIRST
before
running

Sloped
entry~
hit it
right or
pay the
price!

Ⓟ 65
m

Private
Property

Possible to
line this
shore when
levels
permit.

Ⓔ

Ⓔ

Series
of low
ledges

Ⓔ

BLACK

Ⓟ 50m
PINE CHUTES - DO NOT RUN!
~very scenic, cascading falls;
carry over on river left or liftover
the sloped rocks. Pretty campsite.

△

CI~50m. Down the middle

ECO-FACT
A 55-hp Rotax Skidoo
engine running at one-
half horsepower emits the
same carbon dioxide as
121 cars, the nitrous
oxide of .7 cars, and the
hydrocarbons of 328 cars.

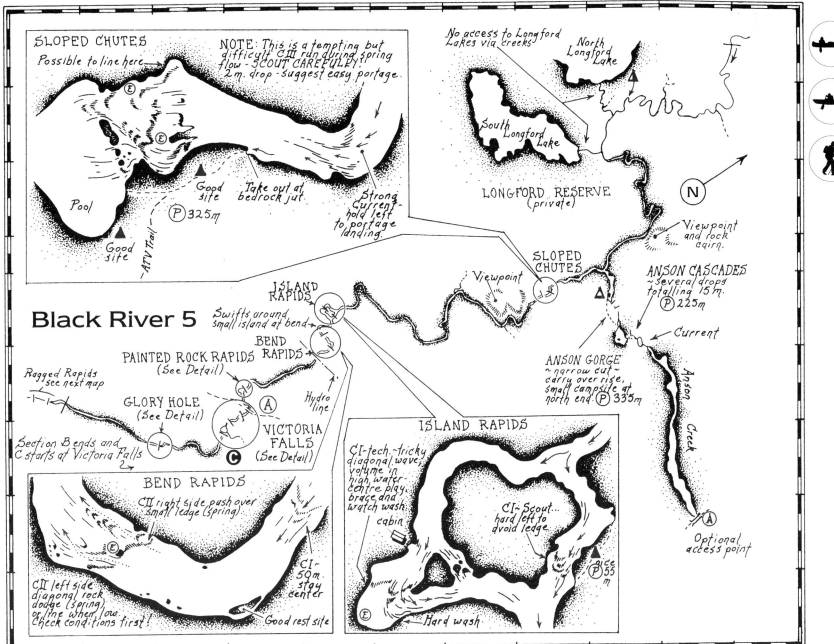

SLOPED CHUTES

Possible to line here

NOTE: This is a tempting but difficult CIII run during spring flow - SCOUT CAREFULLY! 2 m. drop - suggest easy portage.

Pool

Good site

Good site

ATV Trail

(P) 325m

Take out at bedrock jut.

Strong Current - hold left to portage landing.

No access to Longford Lakes via creeks

North Longford Lake

South Longford Lake

LONGFORD RESERVE (private)

(N)

Viewpoint and rock cairn.

Viewpoint

SLOPED CHUTES

ANSON CASCADES ~ several drops totalling 15 m. (P) 225m

Current

Black River 5

ISLAND RAPIDS

Swifts around small island at bend

BEND RAPIDS

PAINTED ROCK RAPIDS (See Detail)

Ragged Rapids see next map

GLORY HOLE (See Detail)

Section B ends and C starts at Victoria Falls

Hydro line

(A)

VICTORIA FALLS (See Detail)

(C)

ANSON GORGE ~ narrow cut ~ carry over rise, small campsite at north end. (P) 335m

Anson Creek

BEND RAPIDS

CII right side push over small ledge (spring)

CII left side diagonal rock dodge (spring) or line when low. check conditions first!

(E)

CI~ 50 m. stay center

Good rest site

ISLAND RAPIDS

CI-tech.~tricky diagonal wave, volume in high water centre play, brace and watch wash.

cabin

CI~ Scout... hard left to avoid ledge

CI~ Scout... hard left to avoid ledge

(E)

Hard wash

nice (P) 55 m

(A)

Optional access point

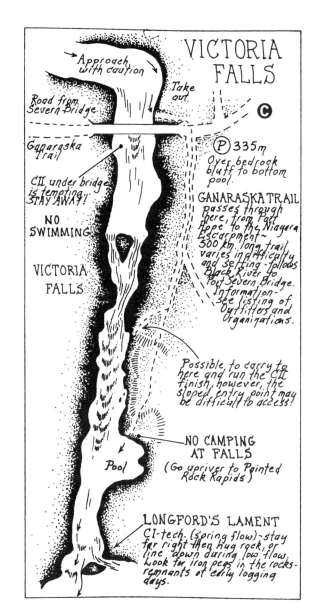

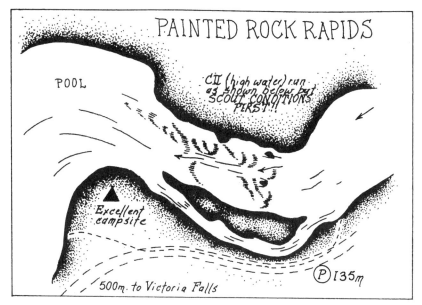

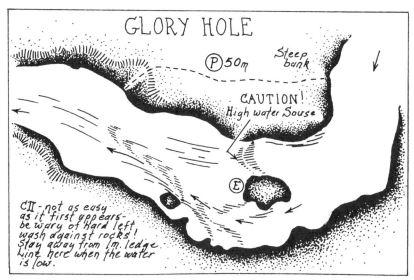

Black River 6

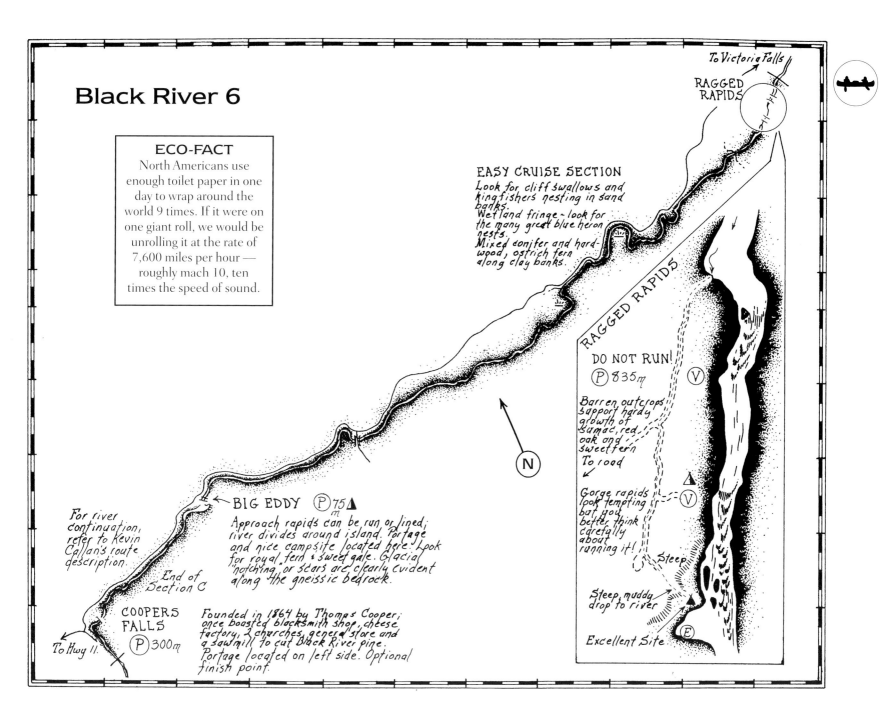

To Victoria Falls

RAGGED RAPIDS

EASY CRUISE SECTION
Look for cliff swallows and kingfishers nesting in sand banks.
Wetland fringe - look for the many great blue heron nests.
Mixed conifer and hardwood, ostrich fern along clay banks.

RAGGED RAPIDS

DO NOT RUN!
Ⓟ 835 m   Ⓥ

Barren outcrops support hardy growth of sumac, red oak and sweet fern

To road

Ⓝ

Gorge rapids look tempting but you better think carefully about running it!

Ⓥ

Steep

BIG EDDY   Ⓟ 75 m ▲

Approach rapids can be run or lined; river divides around island. Portage and nice campsite located here. Look for royal fern & sweet gale. Glacial notching, or scars are clearly evident along the gneissic bedrock.

For river continuation, refer to Kevin Callan's route description.

End of Section C

Steep, muddy drop to river

COOPERS FALLS
Ⓟ 300 m

To Hwy 11.

Founded in 1864 by Thomas Cooper; once boasted blacksmith shop, cheese factory, 2 churches, general store and a sawmill to cut Black River pine. Portage located on left side. Optional finish point.

Ⓔ
Excellent Site

OXTONGUE RIVER
The Hog's Trough

CLASSIFICATION Oxtongue Lake to Marsh's Falls, experienced intermediate to expert; Marsh's Falls to Dwight is novice. *Note: Oxtongue Lake to Hunter's Bridge is intermediate.*

DISTANCE total 18 km (13 km to Marsh's Falls)

TIME 3 to 5 hours (with scouting) to Marsh's Falls; another 1.5 hours to Dwight

SEASON April through August (whitewater section); through October for the last stretch to Dwight

ELEVATION DROP 45 m (whitewater section drops 3 m/km)

CAMPSITES 1 possible site at Key to Algonquin campgrounds

RAPIDS & FALLS 4 CIs, 11 CIIs, 2 CIIIs, 3 waterfalls/chutes

PORTAGES 4 portages (425 m)

MAPS 31 E/7, 31 E/6

ACCESS Highway 60 at Oxtongue Lake or Algonquin Outfitters

TAKE-OUT Town of Dwight (whitewaterists may want to get out at Highway 35)

SPECIALIZED GEAR strictly ABS/Royalex whitewater boats and kayaks for whitewater sections; wetsuits for spring runs

WHITEWATER CHARACTERISTICS & GENERAL HAZARDS
This is certainly a hotspot for whitewaterists. The steep pitch of the river over such a short distance creates the right energy for pool and drop play; there are lots of eddy pools, ledges and wave action to tantalize the adrenaline crowd. Levels are variable throughout the season, becoming more technical by early summer. Long sets of boulder gardens appear as teeth in a gaping jaw as water levels decline, making runs more exciting and dangerous, fast and spirited. Definitely not for the neophyte!

ECOLOGY The Oxtongue is by no means as remote as it is wild, but it is undeveloped. The river has a split personality: it announces its presence in a brash and showy way but is also placid and calm. It is beautiful, to say the least, and has a particular naturalness that typifies more remote Shield-type rivers. Nature seekers not wielding a wide-bladed paddle should start their trip at Marsh's Falls. Here they can experience a "low-energy" delta habitat that defies description.

This is the Lower Oxtongue Heritage Area, undeveloped and scenic, with ample places to view wildlife (68 species of birds, 5 mammals, 8 amphibians and 181 native vascular plants and 2 rare species at that!). The isolated kettle pond near the mouth of the delta has matured into a floating bog-mat fringed with buckbean.

FEATURES An old cantilever footbridge once marked the end of the Bobcaygeon pioneer road. It's known as Hunter's Bridge, after pioneer hellraiser Isaac Hunter, who brought his family north to homestead in the 1860s after fleeing the rebellion of 1837. Falling upon hard times, Isaac died of starvation during one particularly long winter. His wife and daughter survived the ordeal, delirious and almost insane — they trapped and ate the mice that were feeding on his corpse. History has its sad realities. Hunter's Bridge is now a drop-off and pick-up point for those budding paddlers practising their skills on the upper stretch. Those proceeding below the bridge had better have their technique down to a fine art. From Highway 35 at Marsh's Falls, the site of George F. Marsh's sawmill in 1877, novice canoeists can dip their paddles in the relative calm of the Oxtongue delta. One of the spectacles is the Hog's Trough. Composed of tilted gneissic bands of rock and brought to life by the rush of white water, it is one of the most impressive chutes in Muskoka.

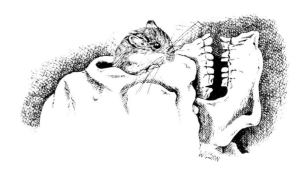

Oxtongue River 1

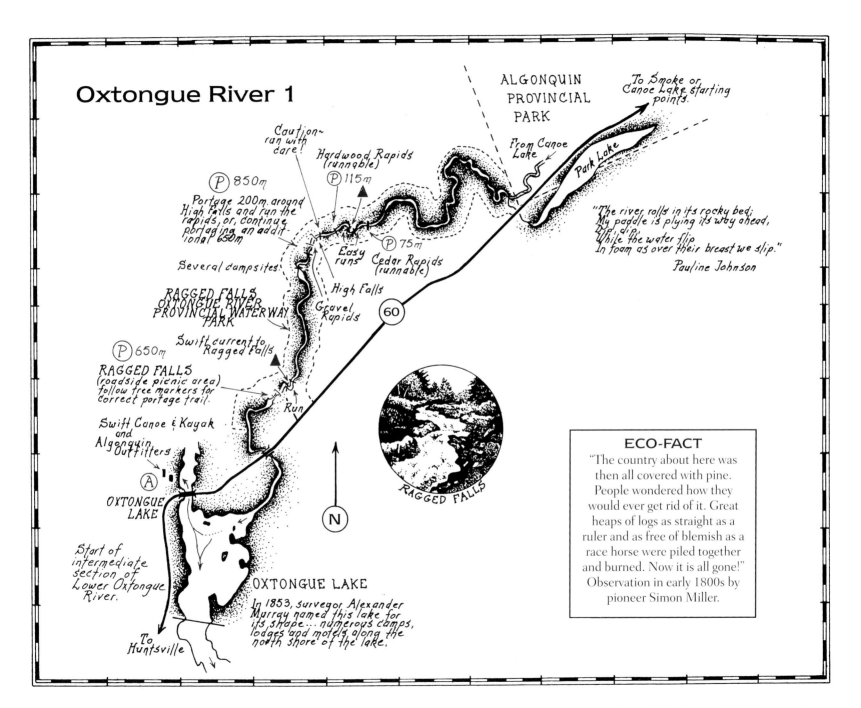

ALGONQUIN PROVINCIAL PARK

To Smoke or Canoe Lake starting points.

From Canoe Lake

Park Lake

Caution~ run with care!

Hardwood Rapids (runnable)

(P) 850m

(P) 115m

Portage 200m. around High Falls and run the rapids, or, continue portaging an additional 650m

"The river rolls in its rocky bed;
My paddle is plying its way ahead,
Dip, dip,
While the water flip
In foam as over their breast we slip."

Pauline Johnson

(P) 75m

Easy runs

Cedar Rapids (runnable)

Several campsites

High Falls

RAGGED FALLS
OXTONGUE RIVER
PROVINCIAL WATERWAY
PARK

Gravel Rapids

60

Swift current to Ragged Falls

(P) 650m

RAGGED FALLS
(roadside picnic area)
follow tree markers for
correct portage trail.

Run

RAGGED FALLS

Swift Canoe & Kayak
and
Algonquin
Outfitters

(A)

OXTONGUE
LAKE

N

ECO-FACT
"The country about here was then all covered with pine. People wondered how they would ever get rid of it. Great heaps of logs as straight as a ruler and as free of blemish as a race horse were piled together and burned. Now it is all gone!" Observation in early 1800s by pioneer Simon Miller.

Start of intermediate section of Lower Oxtongue River.

OXTONGUE LAKE

In 1853, surveyor Alexander Murray named this lake for its shape... numerous camps, lodges and motels along the north shore of the lake.

To Huntsville

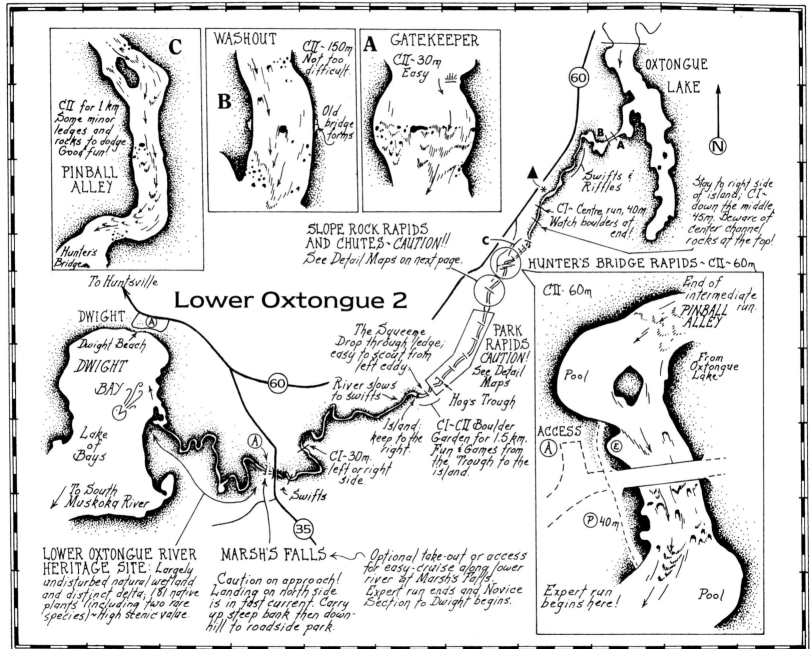

C

CII for 1 km. Some minor ledges and rocks to dodge. Good fun!

PINBALL ALLEY

Hunter's Bridge

WASHOUT

B

CII ~ 150m Not too difficult.

Old bridge forms

A GATEKEEPER

CII ~ 30m Easy

OXTONGUE LAKE

60

N

Swifts & Riffles

CI ~ Centre run, 40m. Watch boulders at end!

Stay to right side of island; CI ~ down the middle, 45m. Beware of center channel rocks at the top!

SLOPE ROCK RAPIDS AND CHUTES ~ CAUTION!! See Detail Maps on next page.

C

HUNTER'S BRIDGE RAPIDS ~ CII ~ 60m

CII ~ 60m

End of intermediate run. PINBALL ALLEY

Lower Oxtongue 2

To Huntsville

DWIGHT A

Dwight Beach

DWIGHT BAY

Lake of Bays

To South Muskoka River

60

The Squeeme Drop through ledge; easy to scout from left eddy.

River slows to swifts

Island keep to the right.

PARK RAPIDS CAUTION! See Detail Maps

Hog's Trough

CI ~ CII Boulder Garden for 1.5 km. Fun & Games from the 'Trough to the island.

Pool

From Oxtongue Lake

ACCESS A

E

P 40m

Expert run begins here!

Pool

A

CI ~ 30m. left or right side

Swifts

35

MARSH'S FALLS

Optional take-out or access for easy-cruise along lower river at Marsh's Falls. Expert run ends and Novice Section to Dwight begins.

LOWER OXTONGUE RIVER HERITAGE SITE: Largely undisturbed natural wetland and distinct delta; 181 native plants (including two rare species)~High scenic value.

Caution on approach! Landing on north side is in fast current. Carry up steep bank then down-hill to roadside park.

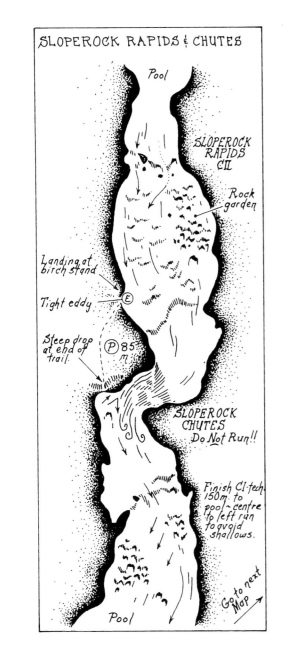

SLOPEROCK RAPIDS & CHUTES

Pool

SLOPEROCK RAPIDS CII

Rock garden

Landing at birch stand

Tight eddy Ⓔ

Steep drop at end of trail. Ⓟ 85 m

SLOPEROCK CHUTES Do Not Run!!

Finish CI-tech 150m. to pool ~ centre to left run to avoid shallows.

Go to next Map

Pool

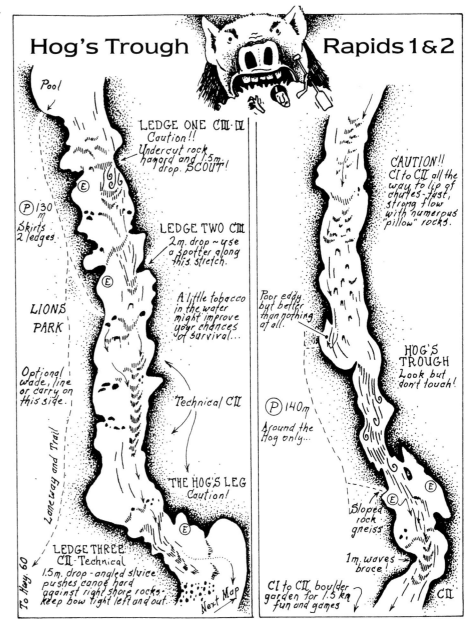

Hog's Trough   Rapids 1 & 2

Pool

LEDGE ONE CIII-IV Caution!! Undercut rock hazard and 1.5m. drop. SCOUT!

Ⓔ

Ⓟ 130 m Skirts 2 ledges

LEDGE TWO CIII 2m. drop ~ use a spotter along this stretch.

Ⓔ

LIONS PARK

A little tobacco in the water might improve your chances of survival...

Optional wade, line or carry on this side.

Technical CII

Laneway and Trail

To Hwy. 60

THE HOG'S LEG Caution!

Ⓔ

LEDGE THREE CII-Technical 1.5m. drop - angled sluice pushes canoe hard against right shore rocks - keep bow tight left and out.

Next Map

CAUTION!! CI to CII all the way to lip of chutes - fast, strong flow with numerous "pillow" rocks.

Poor eddy but better than nothing at all.

HOG'S TROUGH Look but don't touch!

Ⓟ 140m Around the Hog only...

Ⓔ

Sloped rock gneiss

1m. waves brace!

CI to CII boulder garden for 1.5 km fun and games

CII

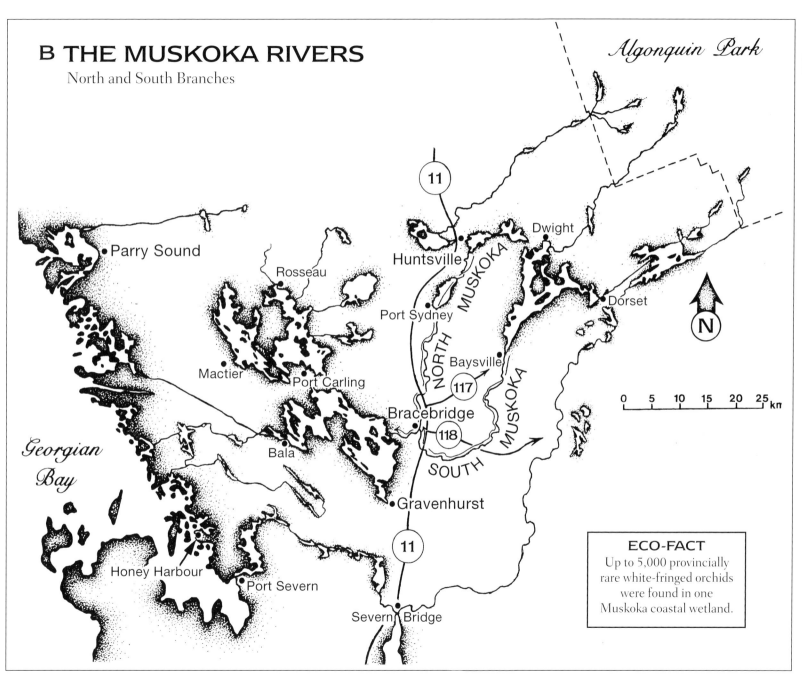

B THE MUSKOKA RIVERS
North and South Branches

Algonquin Park

11

Dwight

Huntsville

Parry Sound

Rosseau

Port Sydney

Mactier

Baysville

NORTH MUSKOKA

117

Port Carling

Bracebridge

118

SOUTH MUSKOKA

Bala

Dorset

N

0 5 10 15 20 25
кп

Georgian Bay

Gravenhurst

11

Honey Harbour

Port Severn

Severn Bridge

ECO-FACT
Up to 5,000 provincially
rare white-fringed orchids
were found in one
Muskoka coastal wetland.

NORTH MUSKOKA RIVER
THE HEART OF MUSKOKA

The North Muskoka is divided into three sections for easy reference: (A) Huntsville to Port Sydney, (B) Port Sydney to High Falls, (C) High Falls to Bracebridge.

CLASSIFICATION (A) novice, (B) experienced novice (avoiding all whitewater), (C) novice

DISTANCE (A) 20 km, (B) 20 km, (C) 8 km

TIME (A) and (B) 4.5 to 6.5 hours, (C) 1.5 to 2 hours

SEASON April through October

ELEVATION DROP 60 m

CAMPSITES one small site; several inns, lodges and B & Bs along the route

RAPIDS & FALLS 4 rapids and 3 falls, with some sections of swifts

PORTAGES 6 (510 m)

MAPS 31 E/3, 31 E/6

ACCESS (A) Huntsville, (B) Port Sydney Dam, (C) High Falls picnic area

TAKE-OUT (A) Port Sydney Beach, (B) High Falls picnic area, (C) Bracebridge Falls

SPECIALIZED GEAR none

WHITEWATER CHARACTERISTICS & GENERAL HAZARDS
Aside from a few novelty swifts and gravel shallows there are no navigable rapids, except for those runs designated as CIIIs on the IRGS scale. Balsam and Duck Chutes are both runnable (if clear of sweepers) but require scouting, close inspection and on-shore safety spotters. Flow varies considerably throughout the season but shouldn't ever hamper easy navigation. Hazards may include having to deal with strong prevailing headwinds on Mary Lake and strong current near portage landings at falls and rapids during high flow periods.

ECOLOGY Many ecological factors here are associated with shoreline deposits left behind by glacial Lake Algonquin. Sand, clay and gravel-based soils are generally deep, but overall, the North Muskoka is undeveloped and marked by remnant pine along the banks, highlighted by Precambrian rock outcrops, mixed with occasional wetlands. Forests are generally a mixture of white spruce, fir, hemlock, pine, white and yellow birch, black cherry and sugar maple, providing a significant natural corridor for the movement of wildlife and plant species. New England sedge, nodding trillium, bloodroot, melic grass, marsh marigold and bayonet rush all grow communally on the fine-textured soils.

FEATURES The upper river, (A), is perfect for kayak touring, with easy access to great lodging and the "softer" side of adventure, but without compromising scenic or ecological rewards. The remainder of the river affords one of the best day outings in Muskoka. Portages are short and the scenic vistas spectacular at three of Muskoka's favourite waterfalls — High Falls, Wilson Falls and Bracebridge Falls. High Falls, known as the Niagara of the North, plunges 14.6 m over gneissic ledges and is best viewed under the glow of evening light.

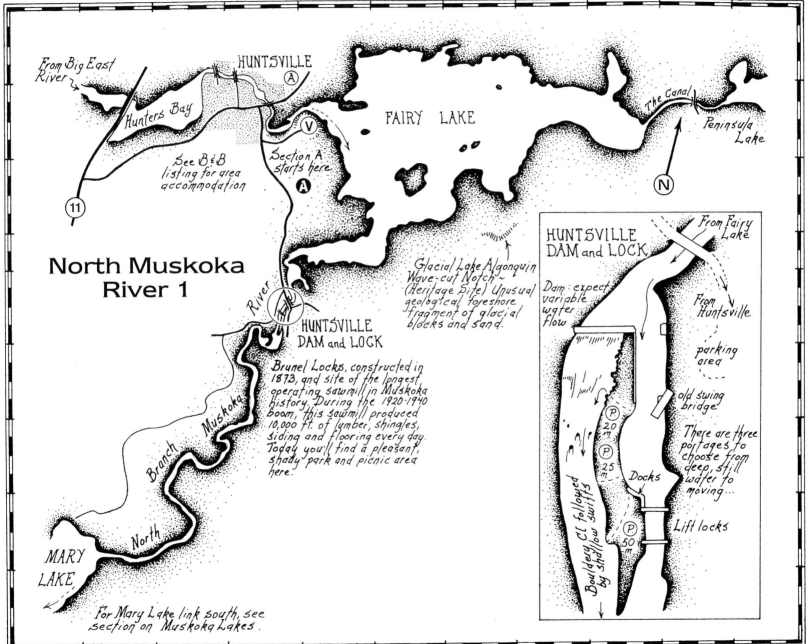

North Muskoka River 1

From Big East River

HUNTSVILLE

Ⓐ

Hunters Bay

FAIRY LAKE

The Canal

Peninsula Lake

Ⓥ

Section A starts here

See B&B listing for area accommodation

Ⓐ

Ⓝ

11

Glacial Lake Algonquin Wave-cut Notch ~ (Heritage Site) Unusual geological foreshore fragment of glacial blocks and sand.

River

Muskoka

LOCK

HUNTSVILLE DAM and LOCK

Brunel Locks, constructed in 1873, and site of the longest operating sawmill in Muskoka history. During the 1920-1940 boom, this sawmill produced 10,000 ft. of lumber, shingles, siding and flooring every day. Today you'll find a pleasant, shady park and picnic area here.

Branch

North

MARY LAKE

For Mary Lake link south, see section on Muskoka Lakes.

HUNTSVILLE DAM and LOCK

From Fairy Lake

Dam: expect variable water flow

From Huntsville

parking area

old swing bridge

Ⓟ 20 m

Ⓟ 25 m

Docks

Ⓟ 50 m

Boulder Cl followed by shallow swifts

There are three portages to choose from deep, still water to moving...

Lift locks

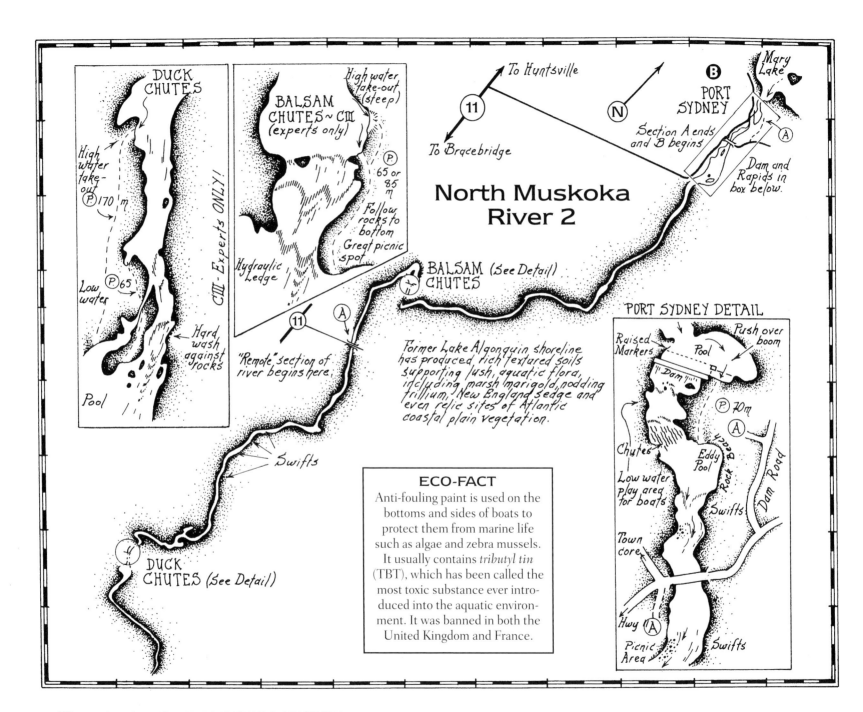

North Muskoka River 3

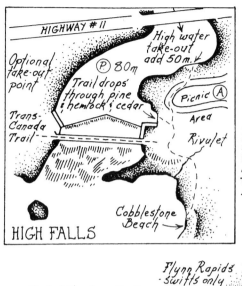

HIGHWAY # 11

Optional take-out point

Trans-Canada Trail

Trail drops through pine & hemlock & cedar

(P) 80m

High water take-out add 50 m. ↓

Picnic (A) Area

Rivulet

Cobblestone Beach →

HIGH FALLS

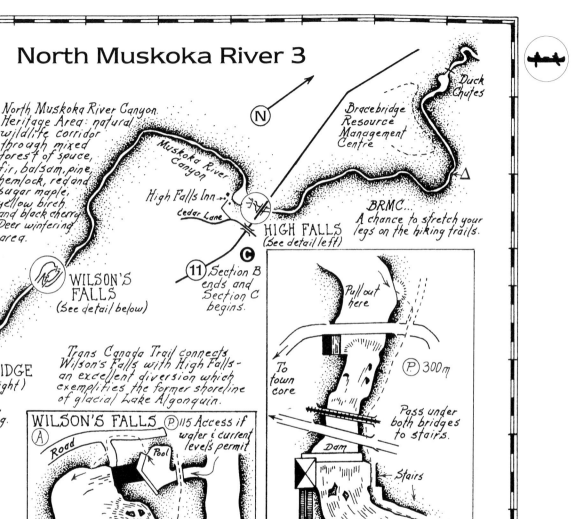

North Muskoka River Canyon Heritage Area: natural wildlife corridor through mixed forest of spruce, fir, balsam, pine, hemlock, red and sugar maple, yellow birch and black cherry. Deer wintering area.

Muskoka River Canyon

High Falls Inn

Cedar Lane

(N)

Bracebridge Resource Management Centre

Duck Chutes

△

BRMC...
A chance to stretch your legs on the hiking trails.

HIGH FALLS
(See detail left)

(11) Section B ends and Section C begins.

(C)

Flynn Rapids - swifts only

WILSON'S FALLS
(See detail below)

End of Section C ↘

To Lake Muskoka, Moon and Musquash River.

BRACEBRIDGE
(See detail right)

For accommodations, refer to B&B listing.

Trans Canada Trail connects Wilson's Falls with High Falls - an excellent diversion which exemplifies the former shoreline of glacial Lake Algonquin.

WILSON'S FALLS

(A) Road

Pool

(P) 115 Access if water & current levels permit

Swifts

Caution here

(P) 230 or 180 m

Bracebridge 2 km.

T.C.T.

BRACEBRIDGE FALLS

Pull out here

To town core

(P) 300m

Pass under both bridges to stairs.

Dam

Stairs

Power House

SOUTH MUSKOKA RIVER
THE EXPLORER'S HIGHWAY

The South Muskoka is separated into three sections for easy reference: **Ⓐ** Baysville to Fraserburg, **Ⓑ** Fraserburg to South Falls, **Ⓒ** South Falls to Bracebridge.

CLASSIFICATION **Ⓐ** and **Ⓑ** novice to intermediate, depending on whitewater skills; **Ⓒ** novice

DISTANCE **Ⓐ** 13 km, **Ⓑ** 28.5 km, **Ⓒ** 6 km

TIME **Ⓐ** 4 to 5 hours, **Ⓑ** 6 to 8.5 hours, **Ⓒ** 1.5 to 2 hours

SEASON April through early November

ELEVATION DROP 90 m

CAMPSITES **Ⓐ** 4 sites, **Ⓑ** 3 sites, **Ⓒ** 2 sites (Bracebridge)

RAPIDS & FALLS **Ⓐ** 6 rapids (3 runnable plus swifts), **Ⓑ** 3 rapids (1 runnable), 4 falls, **Ⓒ** 1 falls

PORTAGES **Ⓐ** 5 (380 m); **Ⓑ** 6 (875 m), but can be reduced to 5 (515 m); **Ⓒ** 1 (475 m) at South Falls

MAPS 31 E/3, 31 D/14

ACCESS **Ⓐ** Baysville Dam, **Ⓑ** Fraserburg village, **Ⓒ** South Falls (east side of Highway 11)

TAKE-OUT **Ⓐ** Fraserburg village, **Ⓑ** picnic area above falls via South Falls Road, **Ⓒ** Bracebridge

SPECIALIZED GEAR wetsuits, helmets, safety gear and playboats for any early-season whitewater runs

WHITEWATER CHARACTERISTICS & GENERAL HAZARDS
There are several choice rapids to run along this route, some that require advanced technical skills and close scrutiny. This is one of Muskoka's best rivers, in which both the novice and the technical river adventurer can parley with the river gods. Water levels are key to the ease of running rapids, but for the average neophyte, anytime is a good time to paddle the river. Risks in touring the South Muskoka River come from running rapids above a prescribed skill level. During high water, paddlers must also be wary of strong current near the tops of rapids and chutes, close to the portage take-outs.

ECOLOGY The South Muskoka River shares much of the same ecological profile as its sister branch to the northwest. Keep a lookout for kingfisher, herons, great horned owls and mergansers. The extensive wetlands along the lower course, especially at Spring Creek, provide a bounty of herb-rich swamp and forest communities.

FEATURES The most notable explorer to push his canoe upstream on this river was none other than David Thompson. In 1837, the Canadian government contracted Thompson, then in his golden years, to search out a canal route between Georgian Bay and the Ottawa River. This was eleven years after Lieutenant Henry Briscoe of the Royal Engineers had already been up the river looking for the same thing. They didn't find one, of course, but they did leave us with some interesting journal notes, sketches and maps.

Although the river can be paddled upstream, something those wishing to explore section **Ⓒ** of the river will need to do, the recommended trip is to drift with the gentle current downstream. The river is surprisingly pristine, despite the few riverside cottages (hails from weekend cottagers on lofty decks offering cold beer and salutations are guaranteed), and the South Muskoka seems far more remote than it actually is. South Falls, once known as Grand or Muskoka Falls, is certainly a hallmark wonder of the Muskoka River watershed. This picturesque chute, even though almost strangled by highway overpass, water flumes, road and hydro plant, is actually quite endearing and lovely to explore. It's easy to comprehend why this falls and canyon below have been a favourite motif for paintbrush and pen for over a century. As part of the historic Peterson Road, the Falls became an established community in 1862. With the cutting of the great pine forests came the need to build a 300 m log slide around the falls to facilitate the timber drives. Part of the log works is still visible along the trail skirting the chasm.

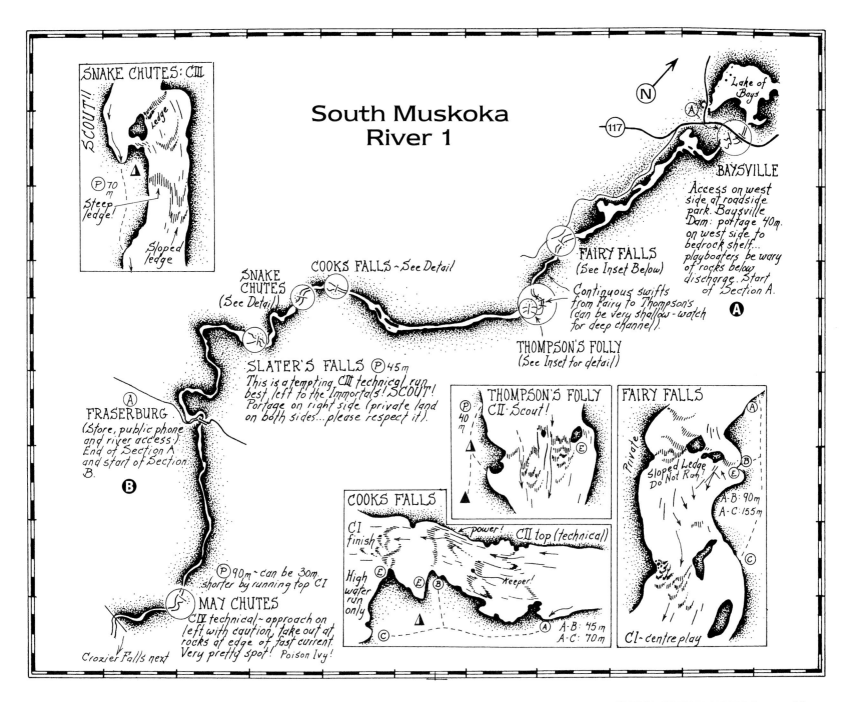

South Muskoka River 1

SNAKE CHUTES: CIII

SCOUT!!

Ledge

P 70 m

Steep ledge!

Sloped ledge

N

Lake of Bays

117

Ⓐ

BAYSVILLE

Access on west side at roadside park. Baysville Dam: portage 40m on west side to bedrock shelf... playboaters be wary of rocks below discharge. Start of Section A.

Ⓐ

FAIRY FALLS
(See Inset Below)

Continuous swifts from Fairy to Thompson's (can be very shallow ~ watch for deep channel).

THOMPSON'S FOLLY
(See Inset for detail)

COOKS FALLS ~ See Detail

SNAKE CHUTES
(See Detail)

SLATER'S FALLS P 45m

This is a tempting CIII technical run best left to the Immortals! SCOUT! Portage on right side (private land on both sides... please respect it).

Ⓐ

FRASERBURG

(Store, public phone and river access.) End of Section A and start of Section B.

Ⓑ

P 90m ~ can be 30m shorter by running top CI

MAY CHUTES

CIV technical~ approach on left with caution, take out at rocks at edge of fast current. Very pretty spot! Poison Ivy!

Crozier Falls next

THOMPSON'S FOLLY
CII: Scout!

P 40 m

Ⓔ

FAIRY FALLS

Ⓐ

Private

Sloped Ledge Do Not Run!

Ⓑ

Ⓔ

A-B: 90m
A-C: 155m

Ⓒ

CI - centre play

COOKS FALLS

CI finish

power!

CII top (technical)

Ⓔ

Ⓔ

Ⓑ

Keeper!

High water run only

Ⓐ

Ⓒ

A-B: 45m
A-C: 70m

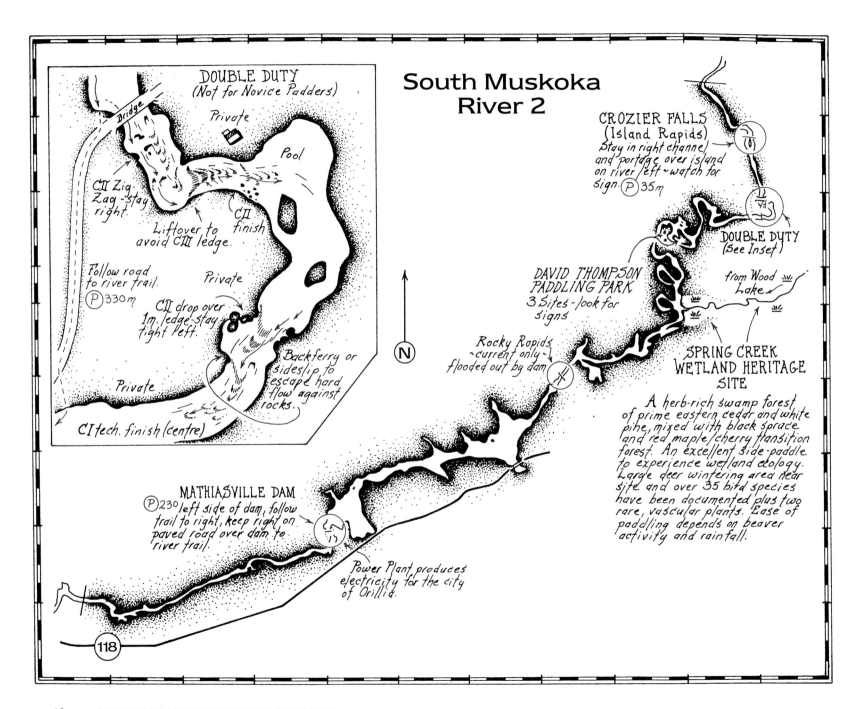

South Muskoka River 2

DOUBLE DUTY
(Not for Novice Padders)

Private

Pool

Bridge

CII Zig Zag - stay right.

CII finish

Liftover to avoid CIII ledge.

Follow road to river trail.
Ⓟ 330m

Private

CII drop over 1m ledge - stay tight left.

Backferry or sideslip to escape hard flow against rocks.

Private

CI tech. finish (centre)

CROZIER FALLS
(Island Rapids)
Stay in right channel and portage over island on river left - watch for sign. Ⓟ 35m

DOUBLE DUTY
(See Inset)

from Wood Lake

DAVID THOMPSON PADDLING PARK
3 Sites - look for signs

Rocky Rapids - current only - flooded out by dam

SPRING CREEK WETLAND HERITAGE SITE

A herb-rich swamp forest of prime eastern cedar and white pine, mixed with black spruce and red maple/cherry transition forest. An excellent side-paddle to experience wetland ecology. Large deer wintering area near site and over 35 bird species have been documented plus two rare, vascular plants. Ease of paddling depends on beaver activity and rainfall.

MATHIASVILLE DAM
Ⓟ 230 left side of dam, follow trail to right, keep right on paved road over dam to river trail.

Power Plant produces electricity for the city of Orillia.

118

Ⓝ

South Muskoka River 3

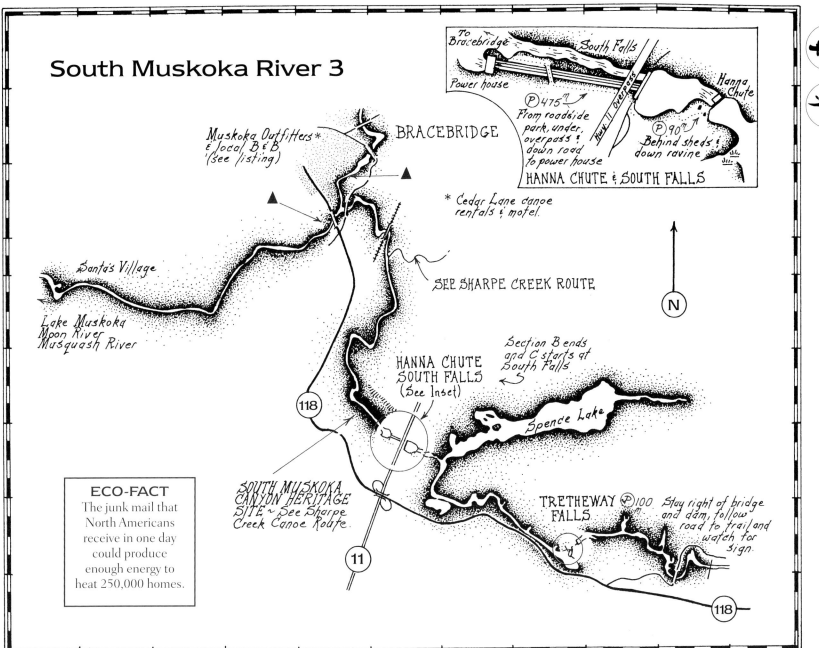

Muskoka Outfitters *
& local B&B
(see listing)

BRACEBRIDGE

* Cedar Lane canoe
rentals & motel.

Santa's Village

Lake Muskoka
Moon River
Musquash River

SEE SHARPE CREEK ROUTE

HANNA CHUTE
SOUTH FALLS
(See Inset)

Section B ends
and C starts at
South Falls

Spence Lake

118

SOUTH MUSKOKA
CANYON HERITAGE
SITE ~ See Sharpe
Creek Canoe Route.

TRETHEWAY
FALLS

ⓟ100ᵐ Stay right of bridge
and dam, follow
road to trail and
watch for
sign.

11

118

Inset

To
Bracebridge

South Falls

Power house

ⓟ475ᵐ
From roadside
park, under.
overpass &
down road
to power house

Hanna
Chute

Hwy. 11 overpass

ⓟ90ᵐ
Behind sheds &
down ravine

HANNA CHUTE & SOUTH FALLS

N

ECO-FACT
The junk mail that
North Americans
receive in one day
could produce
enough energy to
heat 250,000 homes.

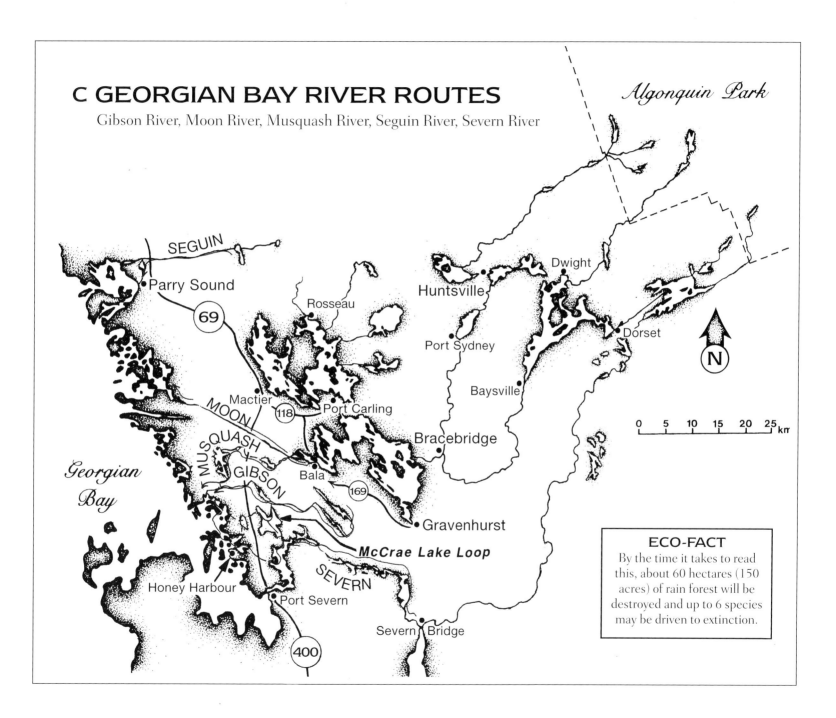

C GEORGIAN BAY RIVER ROUTES

Gibson River, Moon River, Musquash River, Seguin River, Severn River

Algonquin Park

SEGUIN

Parry Sound

(69)

Rosseau

Dwight

Huntsville

Port Sydney

Dorset

N

Mactier

(118)

Port Carling

Baysville

MOON

MUSQUASH

GIBSON

Bala

Bracebridge

0 5 10 15 20 25 km

Georgian Bay

(169)

Gravenhurst

McCrae Lake Loop

Honey Harbour

SEVERN

Port Severn

Severn Bridge

(400)

ECO-FACT
By the time it takes to read this, about 60 hectares (150 acres) of rain forest will be destroyed and up to 6 species may be driven to extinction.

GIBSON RIVER
The Crooked River

Note: Adjoining loops and side trips are listed separate from the river route.

CLASSIFICATION experienced novice

DISTANCE 45 km

TIME 3 easy days

SEASON May through October

ELEVATION DROP 40 m

CAMPSITES 22 (concentration of sites from Gibson Lake to Go Home Lake Dam)

RAPIDS & FALLS 18 rapids (17 CI–CI technical), 7 waterfalls/chutes

PORTAGES 8 (955 m); can be shortened to 785 m by creative river-work

MAPS 31 D/13 (covers river and additional loops)

ACCESS Highway 169 to Torrance, south on Southwood Road 8 km to Nine Mile Lake marina access

TAKE-OUT Go Home Lake marina

WHITEWATER CHARACTERISTICS & GENERAL HAZARDS Rapids are normally shallow, typical of the glacial spillways, and may necessitate lining, wading or portaging if the water levels drop by early summer. Most navigable whitewater is fairly straightforward, with the option to portage. Other hazards include rattlesnakes (keep dogs leashed), poison ivy, and turbulent water and boils below Go Home Lake Dam, especially during peak flow periods.

ECOLOGY Wet meadows, rock barrens, majestic white pines, and the ancient yodel of loons echoing against rock cliffs are all hallmark traits of the Gibson. Significant natural attributes make this corridor unique in many ways: it is home to 18 species of reptiles and amphibians, including the threatened Eastern Massasauga rattlesnake.

FEATURES Clear night skies, a trek along the Gibson Wilderness Trail, running whitewater, bathing under the spray of a 15 m waterfall, many choices for ways to continue the route — all make the Gibson River special.

OPTIONAL ROUTES & LOOPS Gibson, McCrae & McDonald Loop: This 42 km, eight-portage route is one of the most popular Muskoka canoe routes. The McDonald Lake access can be jammed with canoeists on any summer weekend, so I recommend that you consider paddling in the off-season or summer mid-week to avoid the congestion. I have illustrated additional loops that can either be added on to the Gibson Loop or done on their own as a loop from the McDonald Lake access point. (For the North Bay, Buck Lake extension, add 13.5 km and two portages; for the South Bay, Baxter Lake extension, add 27.5 km and two portages.) McCrae has to be one of my favourites, as it is with many ardent paddlers; that's why when the Ontario government sanctioned the construction of a snowmobile bridge over the falls at the entrance to the acclaimed "wilderness reserve," environmentalists and canoeists were outraged. The ecological communities represented here are typically Georgian Bay Coastal and have not been altered from their natural state. The area boasts impressive gneissic rock outcrops and cliffs, and is home of the fox snake, Massasauga rattlesnake, peregrine falcon and prairie warbler. Adventure is not limited to just paddling — the hike from McDonald Lake access to Georgian Bay is one of the best treks in Muskoka! The only fee charged is for overnight camping at Six Mile Lake Provincial Park, should you venture in that direction.

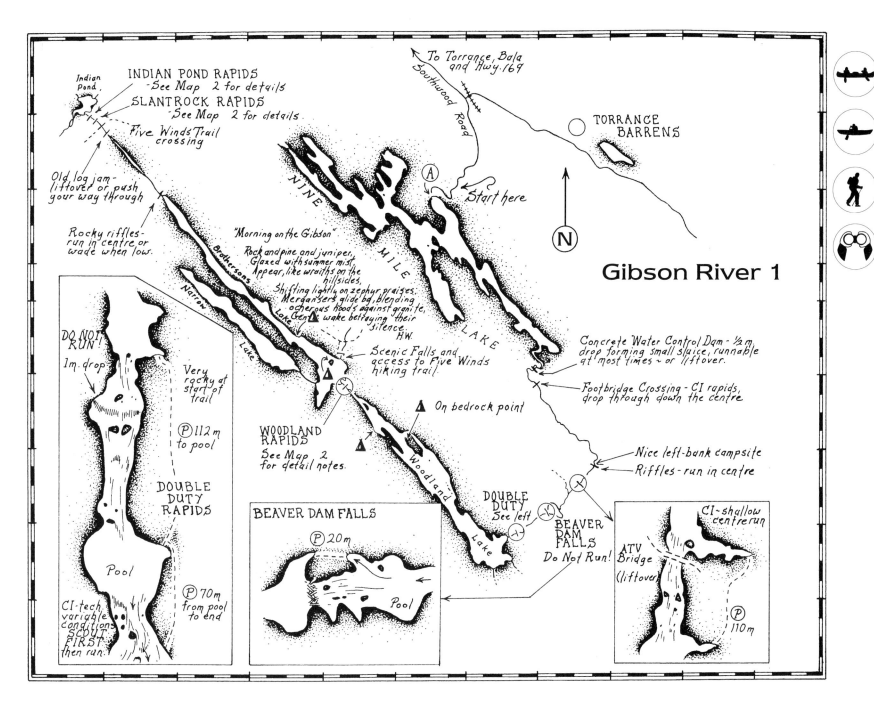

Indian Pond

INDIAN POND RAPIDS
- See Map 2 for details

SLANTROCK RAPIDS
- See Map 2 for details

Five Winds Trail crossing

Old log jam - liftover or push your way through

Rocky riffles - run in centre or wade when low.

To Torrance, Bala and Hwy. 169

Southwood Road

Ⓐ

Start here

TORRANCE BARRENS

Ⓝ

Gibson River 1

NINE MILE LAKE

"Morning on the Gibson"

Rock and pine and juniper,
Glazed with summer mist,
Appear like wraiths on the hillsides,
Shifting lightly on zephyr praises.
Mergansers glide by, blending
ocherous hoods against granite,
Gentle wake betraying their
silence. H.W.

Brothersons

Narrow Lake

Scenic Falls and access to Five Winds hiking trail

Concrete Water Control Dam - ½ m drop forming small sluice, runnable at most times ~ or liftover.

Footbridge Crossing - CI rapids, drop through down the centre

DO NOT RUN!

1m. drop

Very rocky at start of trail

Ⓟ 112 m to pool

DOUBLE DUTY RAPIDS

Pool

CI - tech variable condition. SCOUT FIRST then run.

Ⓟ 70 m from pool to end

△ On bedrock point

△

△

Woodland Lake

WOODLAND RAPIDS
See Map 2 for detail notes.

BEAVER DAM FALLS

Ⓟ 20 m

Pool

Nice left-bank campsite

Riffles - run in centre

DOUBLE DUTY
See left

BEAVER DAM FALLS
Do Not Run!

CI - shallow centre run

ATV Bridge (liftover)

Ⓟ 110 m

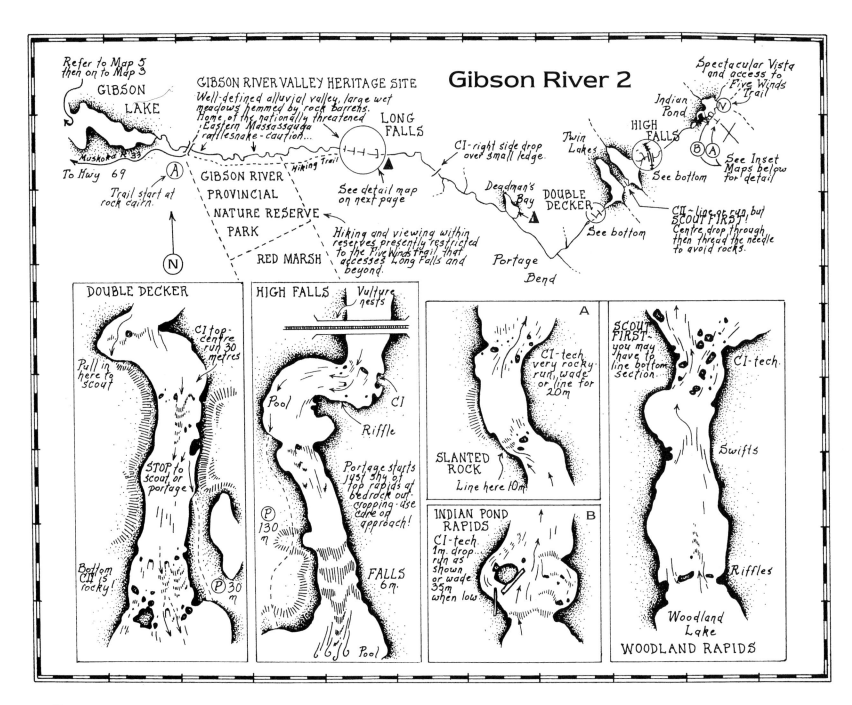

Gibson River 2

Refer to Map 5 then on to Map 3

GIBSON LAKE

Muskoka R. 33

To Hwy 69

Trail start at rock cairn.

GIBSON RIVER VALLEY HERITAGE SITE
Well-defined alluvial valley, large wet meadows hemmed by rock barrens. Home of the nationally threatened Eastern Massassauga rattlesnake - caution...

GIBSON RIVER PROVINCIAL NATURE RESERVE PARK

RED MARSH

Hiking Trail

See detail map on next page

Hiking and viewing within reserves presently restricted to the Five Winds Trail that accesses Long Falls and beyond.

LONG FALLS

CI - right side drop over small ledge.

Deadman's Bay

DOUBLE DECKER

See bottom

Portage Bend

Twin Lakes

HIGH FALLS

See bottom

Spectacular Vista and access to Five Winds Trail

Indian Pond

N

See Inset Maps below for detail

B   A
X

CI - line or run, but SCOUT FIRST! Centre drop through then thread the needle to avoid rocks.

DOUBLE DECKER

CI top-centre run 30 metres

Pull in here to scout

STOP to scout or portage

Bottom CI is rocky!

P 30 m

HIGH FALLS

Vulture nests

Pool

CI

Riffle

Portage starts just shy of top rapids at bedrock outcropping - use care on approach!

P 130 m

FALLS 6 m.

Pool

A

CI - tech very rocky - run, wade or line for 20m

SLANTED ROCK

Line here 10m

INDIAN POND RAPIDS   B

CI - tech. 1m drop - run as shown or wade 35m when low

SCOUT FIRST - you may have to line bottom section

CI - tech

Swifts

Riffles

Woodland Lake

WOODLAND RAPIDS

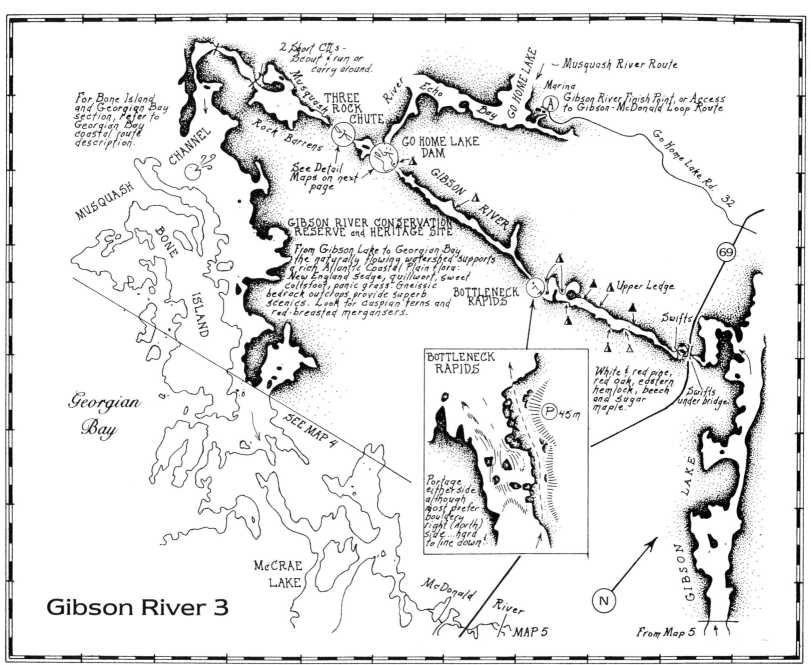

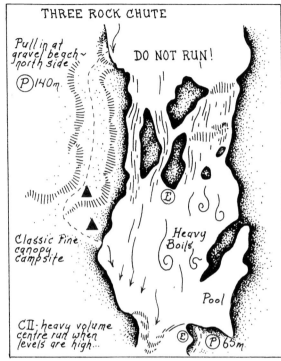

THREE ROCK CHUTE

DO NOT RUN!

Pull in at gravel beach ~ north side

P 140m

Classic Pine canopy campsite

E

Heavy Boils

Pool

CII - heavy volume centre run when levels are high..

E P 65m

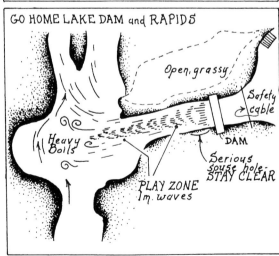

GO HOME LAKE DAM and RAPIDS

Open, grassy

Safety cable

DAM

Heavy Boils

Serious souse hole - STAY CLEAR

PLAY ZONE 1m. waves

ECO-FACT
Earliest ice-out for the major Muskoka Lakes was March 27, 1946; the latest was May 7, 1926 — somewhere in between is the average.

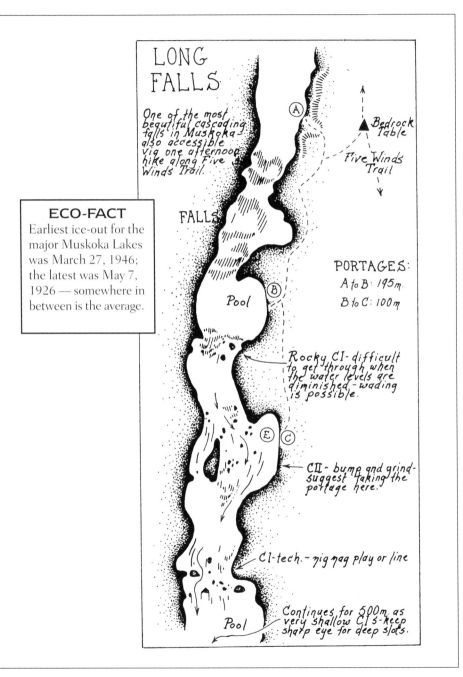

LONG FALLS

One of the most beautiful cascading falls in Muskoka, also accessible via one afternoon hike along Five Winds Trail.

A

Bedrock Table

Five Winds Trail

FALLS

PORTAGES:
A to B: 195m
B to C: 100m

Pool

B

Rocky CI - difficult to get through when the water levels are diminished - wading is possible.

E C

CII - bump and grind - suggest taking the portage here.

CI - tech. - zig zag play or line

Continues for 500m as very shallow CI - keep sharp eye for deep slots.

Pool

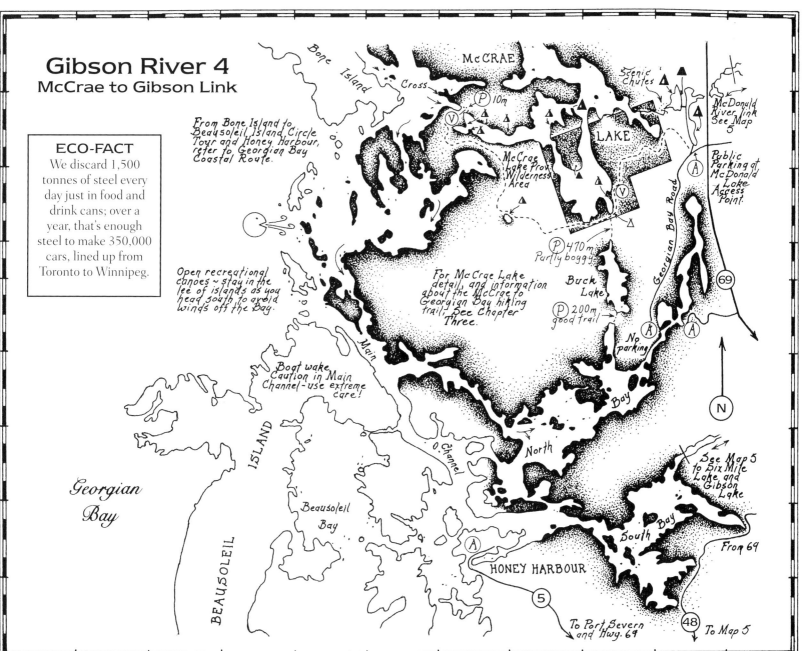

Gibson River 4
McCrae to Gibson Link

ECO-FACT

We discard 1,500 tonnes of steel every day just in food and drink cans; over a year, that's enough steel to make 350,000 cars, lined up from Toronto to Winnipeg.

McCRAE

Scenic Chutes

Bone Island

Cross

P 10m

V

LAKE

McDonald River Link See Map 5

From Bone Island to Beausoleil Island Circle Tour and Honey Harbour, refer to Georgian Bay Coastal Route.

McCrae Lake Prov. Wilderness Area

Public Parking at McDonald Lake Access Point

A

V

Open recreational canoes ~ stay in the lee of islands as you head south to avoid winds off the Bay.

For McCrae Lake detail, and information about the McCrae to Georgian Bay hiking trail, see Chapter Three.

P 470m Partly boggy.

Buck Lake

Georgian Bay Road

69

P 200m good trail

A

A

No parking

A

Main

Boat wake Caution in Main Channel - use extreme care!

O. Channel

North

Bay

N

See Map 5 to Six Mile Lake, and Gibson Lake

Georgian Bay

ISLAND

Beausoleil Bay

South Bay

From 69

A

BEAUSOLEIL

HONEY HARBOUR

5

To Port Severn and Hwy. 69

48 To Map 5

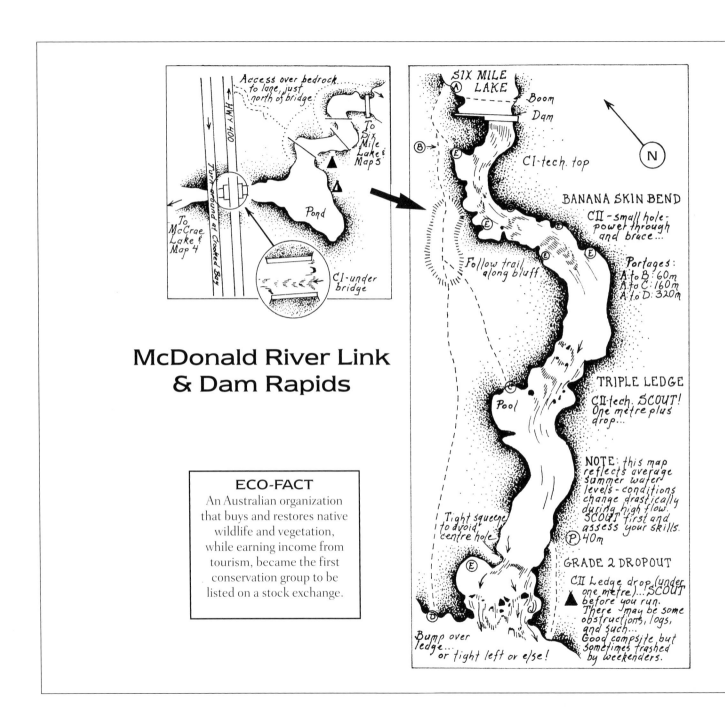

McDonald River Link & Dam Rapids

ECO-FACT

An Australian organization that buys and restores native wildlife and vegetation, while earning income from tourism, became the first conservation group to be listed on a stock exchange.

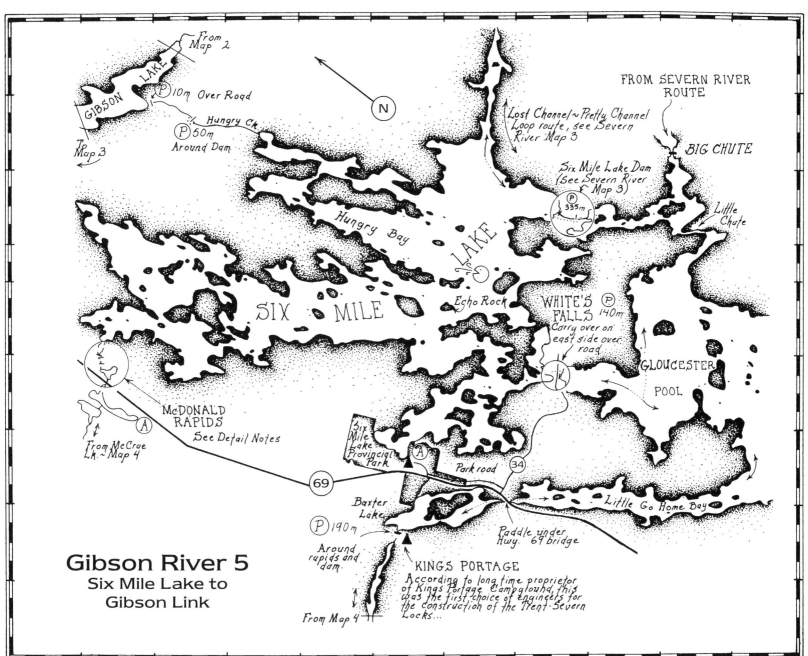

From Map 2

GIBSON LAKE

P 10m Over Road

Hungry Ck.

P 50m Around Dam

To Map 3

N

Hungry Bay

LAKE

FROM SEVERN RIVER ROUTE

Lost Channel ~ Pretty Channel Loop route, see Severn River Map 3

BIG CHUTE

Six Mile Lake Dam (See Severn River Map 3)

P 335m

Little Chute

SIX - MILE

Echo Rock

WHITE'S FALLS

P 140m

Carry over on east side over road

GLOUCESTER POOL

From McCrae Lk ~ Map 4

A

McDONALD RAPIDS

See Detail Notes

Six Mile Lake Provincial Park

A

Park road

34

69

Baxter Lake

Little Go Home Bay

Paddle under Hwy. 69 bridge

P 190m

Around rapids and dam.

KINGS PORTAGE

According to long time proprietor of Kings Portage Campground, this was the first choice of engineers for the construction of the Trent-Severn Locks...

From Map 4

Gibson River 5
Six Mile Lake to Gibson Link

MOON RIVER

Mons zibbi MOOSE RIVER

CLASSIFICATION experienced novice; spring and high water runs, intermediate

DISTANCE Bala to Highway 69, 16.5 km; Highway 69 to Woods Bay, 20.5 km; total 37 km

TIME 3 days

SEASON late May to early October

ELEVATION DROP 48 m

CAMPSITES 16 (concentrations from Curtain Falls to Moon Falls)

RAPIDS & FALLS 1 dam, 10 runnable CI–CIIs, 6 chutes/falls

PORTAGES 8 (1,022 m); longest trail is 385 m

MAP 31 E/4

ACCESS Town of Bala Park (or Ragged Rapids access on the Musquash; see Musquash route)

TAKE-OUT Woods Bay marina, Georgian Bay

FEE parking fee for leaving vehicle at marina

ADDITIONAL RESOURCES *A Paddler's Guide to the Rivers of Ontario and Quebec* by Kevin Callan

SPECIALIZED GEAR wetsuits and ABS canoes for high water and spring runs; wading boots for summer

WHITEWATER CHARACTERISTICS & GENERAL HAZARDS There have been accidents and deaths on the Moon River. The water here can be dangerous to those who lack canoeing savvy. Along the Bala Reach, the full force of the Muskoka watershed unites as a single, powerful entity. During peak flow, when all floodgates are wide open, there is such a fury of water bursting from the Bala control dam that it creates its own wind. Six kilometres downstream, the Moon River splits into two channels — the Moon and the Musquash. It is easy to see how the rapids along the Moon can be wickedly dangerous or passively benign. The river is subject to quick changes in hydrology, especially below the dams, so canoeists must be wary at all times and proceed to each rapid with care. Below Highway 69 the river narrows considerably, allowing little time or room to manoeuvre during high flow. But for the most part, because much of the Moon's flow was diverted over to the Musquash Channel by Ontario Hydro in 1938, the river quickly loses its vitality by early summer and the rapids become choked with rocks. Best time to hit the Moon for whitewater play is mid-flow; monitor the outflow from the Bala Dam or call the local MNR for flow data.

ECOLOGY Because water levels are regulated by hydroelectric installations upriver, the development of a natural shoreline community has been compromised. Nonetheless, the Moon River environs has maintained much of its backshore ecological character and supports a rather significant talus-slope habitat. The lower river, on approach to Moon Falls from Curtain Falls, is absolutely stunning. Spectacular cliffs, abrupt slopes and islands maintain a healthy, mature red and white pine forest. Precambrian ridges support a typical weatherworn, scabrous growth of common juniper and staghorn sumac as you approach Georgian Bay. Where the drift-cover of till is deeper, a successional forest of trembling aspen, red maple, white birch, oak and pine dominates the corridor. Massasauga rattlesnakes are frequently seen at Moon Falls, but generally the river is not a particularly productive corridor for wildlife.

FEATURES The Moon River "valley" was never settled. The steep bedrock ridges and deep bogs made homesteading undesirable and impossible, and they are one of the primary contributing factors to the remote nature of the corridor today. Many people relate the name of the river to the song "Moon River," a favourite of 1950s crooners. But it had little to do with any astronomical or romantic notion; rather, the name of the river was bastardized from *mons*, the Anishnabe word for moose. As early as 1829, history makes note of a particular "moose" river named by early fur traders of the region. The Moon, or Moose River, is not likely to be home to any moose these days but it does portray the personality of Muskoka like no other river. It blends timeless natural beauty with a dangerous charm not to be unnoticed or taken too lightly by adventure seekers. Moon Falls and the pools below may be one of the most picturesque and otherworldly places I have ever chanced upon in my travels.

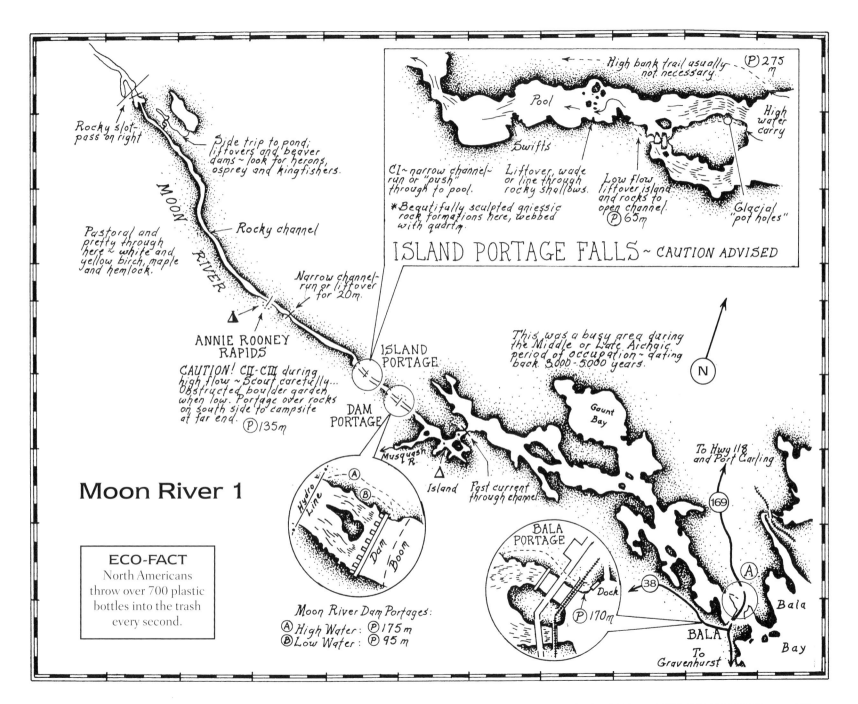

Rocky slot-pass on right

Side trip to pond; liftovers and beaver dams ~ look for herons, osprey and kingfishers.

MOON RIVER

Pastoral and pretty through here ~ white and yellow birch, maple and hemlock.

Rocky channel

Narrow channel- run or liftover for 20m.

ANNIE ROONEY RAPIDS

CAUTION! CII-CIII during high flow ~ Scout carefully... Obstructed boulder garden when low. Portage over rocks on south side to campsite at far end. (P) 135m

Moon River 1

ECO-FACT
North Americans throw over 700 plastic bottles into the trash every second.

High bank trail usually not necessary. (P) 275 m

Pool

Swifts

High water carry

CI ~ narrow channel- run or "push" through to pool.

Liftover, wade or line through rocky shallows.

Low flow liftover island and rocks to open channel. (P) 65m

Glacial "pot holes"

*Beautifully sculpted gneissic rock formations here, webbed with quartz.

ISLAND PORTAGE FALLS ~ CAUTION ADVISED

ISLAND PORTAGE

DAM PORTAGE

Musquash R.

This was a busy area during the Middle or Late Archaic period of occupation ~ dating back 3,000-5,000 years.

N

Gaunt Bay

Island

Fast current through channel

To Hwy 118 and Port Carling

169

Hydro Line

(A)

(B)

Dam

Boom

Moon River Dam Portages:
(A) High Water: (P) 175 m
(B) Low Water: (P) 95 m

BALA PORTAGE

Dock

(P) 170m

38

(A)

Bala

BALA

Bay

To Gravenhurst

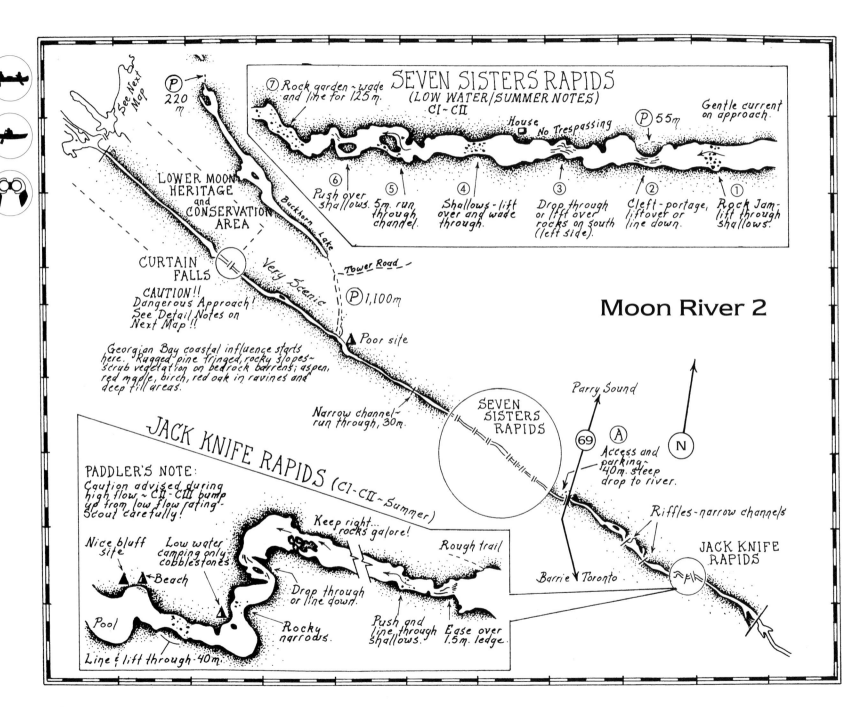

SEVEN SISTERS RAPIDS
(LOW WATER/SUMMER NOTES)
CI~CII

Gentle current on approach.

⑦ Rock garden~wade and line for 125m.

House — No Trespassing

Ⓟ 55m

⑥ Push over shallows.

⑤ 5m. run through channel.

④ Shallows~lift over and wade through.

③ Drop through or lift over rocks on south (left side).

② Cleft~portage, liftover or line down.

① Rock Jam~lift through shallows.

See Next Map

Ⓟ 220m

LOWER MOON HERITAGE and CONSERVATION AREA

Buckhorn Lake

Tower Road

CURTAIN FALLS

Very Scenic

Ⓟ 1,100m

△ Poor site

CAUTION!! Dangerous Approach! See Detail Notes on Next Map!!

Georgian Bay coastal influence starts here. Rugged pine fringed, rocky slopes~ scrub vegetation on bedrock barrens; aspen, red maple, birch, red oak in ravines and deep till areas.

Narrow channel~ run through, 30m.

Moon River 2

Parry Sound

SEVEN SISTERS RAPIDS

69 Ⓐ

Ⓝ

Access and parking~ 140m. steep drop to river.

Riffles~narrow channels

Rough trail

Barrie ▼ Toronto

JACK KNIFE RAPIDS

JACK KNIFE RAPIDS (CI~CII~Summer)

PADDLER'S NOTE:
Caution advised during high flow ~ CII~CIII bump up from low flow rating~ Scout carefully!

Keep right... rocks galore!

Nice bluff site

Low water camping only ~ cobblestones

△ △ Beach

Drop through or line down.

Pool

Rocky narrows.

Push and line through shallows.

Ease over 1.5m. ledge

Line & lift through~40m.

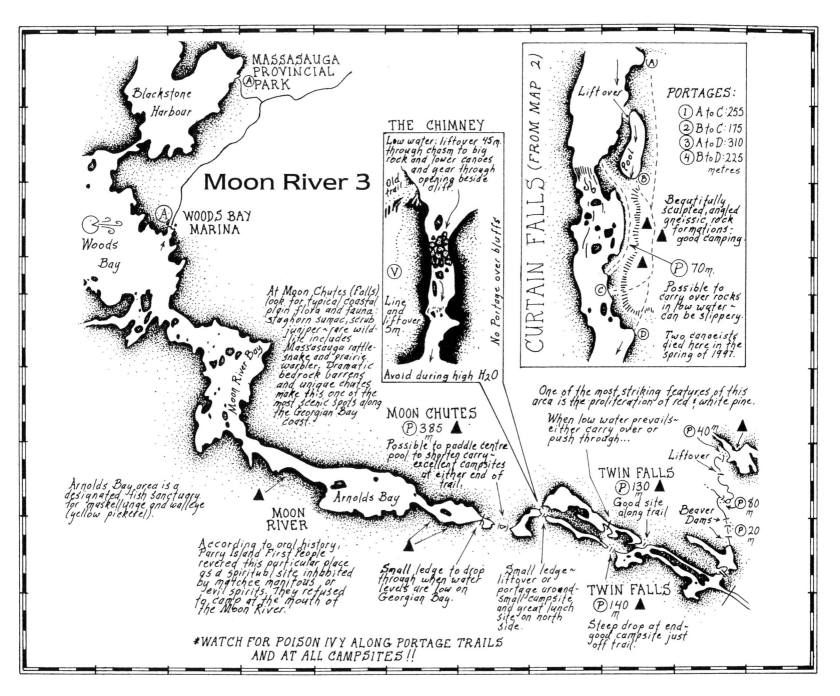

MASSASAUGA PROVINCIAL (A) PARK

Blackstone Harbour

Moon River 3

(A) **WOODS BAY MARINA**

Woods Bay

Moon River Bay

THE CHIMNEY

Low water: liftover 45m through chasm to big rock and lower canoes and gear through opening beside cliff.

old trail

(V)

Line and liftover 5m

Avoid during high H₂O

No Portage over bluffs

CURTAIN FALLS *(FROM MAP 2)*

Lift over

(A)

Pool

(B)

PORTAGES:
1. A to C: 255
2. B to C: 175
3. A to D: 310
4. B to D: 225
metres

Beautifully sculpted, angled gneissic rock formations: good camping

(P) 70m.

(C)

(D)

Possible to carry over rocks in low water ~ can be slippery.

Two canoeists died here in the spring of 1997.

At Moon Chutes (Falls) look for typical coastal plain flora and fauna: staghorn sumac, scrub juniper ~ rare wildlife includes Massasauga rattlesnake and prairie warbler. Dramatic bedrock barrens and unique chutes make this one of the most scenic spots along the Georgian Bay coast.

MOON CHUTES

(P) 385 m ▲

Possible to paddle centre pool to shorten carry ~ excellent campsites at either end of trail.

One of the most striking features of this area is the proliferation of red & white pine.

When low water prevails ~ either carry over or push through...

(P) 40 m ▲

Liftover

TWIN FALLS

(P) 130 ▲

Good site along trail

(P) 80 m

Beaver Dams

(P) 20 m

Arnolds Bay area is a designated fish sanctuary for muskellunge and walleye (yellow pickerel).

MOON RIVER

Arnolds Bay

According to oral history, Parry Island First People revered this particular place as a spiritual site inhabited by matchee manitous or devil spirits. They refused to camp at the mouth of the Moon River.

Small ledge to drop through when water levels are low on Georgian Bay.

Small ledge ~ liftover or portage around ~ small campsite and great lunch site on north side.

TWIN FALLS

(P) 140 m ▲

Steep drop at end ~ good campsite just off trail.

＊WATCH FOR POISON IVY ALONG PORTAGE TRAILS AND AT ALL CAMPSITES!!

MUSQUASH RIVER
GHOSTS AND RIVER RATS

CLASSIFICATION novice
DISTANCE 23.5 km (Ragged Rapids Dam to Go Home Lake marina)
TIME 2 days
SEASON May through October
ELEVATION DROP 28 m
CAMPSITES 25 sites
RAPIDS & FALLS 2 dams, 1 CI rapid, several swifts, 2 chutes/falls
PORTAGES 4 (765 m); longest is 425 m at Sandy Gray Falls
MAPS 31 E/4, 31 D/13
ACCESS Muskoka Road 38 to Ragged Rapids Road; follow to picnic area past dam
TAKE-OUT Go Home Lake Marina (option to continue on to Georgian Bay)
FEE parking vehicle at marina
SPECIALIZED GEAR none
WHITEWATER CHARACTERISTICS & GENERAL HAZARDS
Almost all of the major rapids (as indicated on the topographical map) have been drowned out by the Big Eddy Dam, leaving behind only swifts and current. The rapids leading to Sandy Gray Falls make an excellent but technical and dangerous run — be wary and scout first! Paddlers may encounter some minor problems from prevailing head-winds on Go Home Lake.
ECOLOGY From Ragged Rapids to Big Eddy you'll find at least 50 species of vascular plants including the late-summer bloomers — cardinal flower and golden hedge-hyssop. There are also three rare species — panic grass, Virginia meadow beauty and slender yellow-eyed grass. Below Gray Falls the river supports an unusual white pine — white birch — silver maple bottomland forest (warmer than normal), more usual in southern landscapes. There are 149 recorded species of vascular plants living in the stony sand till and open bedrock knolls. Wetland communities are extensive — from open-water aquatic macrophytes to emergent, herb-rich, rush marshes (look for red-winged blackbirds and bitterns). The name of the river is derived from the Native *musquash*, meaning muskrat, an animal that is frequently seen among the reeds along the shore.
FEATURES The Musquash is a geological anomaly. Veering off the somewhat obvious straight-cut geological notch of the Moon corridor, the river wends its own way to Georgian Bay, drawing most of the flow from Lake Muskoka with it. And although hydro developments have quieted the river from its original vitality, it remains one of the most picturesque rivers in the Muskoka region, and in central Ontario, for that matter. The river and most of the adjoining lake systems remain undeveloped and have many good camping sites. Historically, the Musquash was a major log-drive river. If you are camping at or near Sandy Gray Falls, it is likely that you'll hear or see a ghost walking the shoreline near the chutes. A logger drowned after trying to free a logjam that was backing up the timber coming down the river.

Musquash River 1

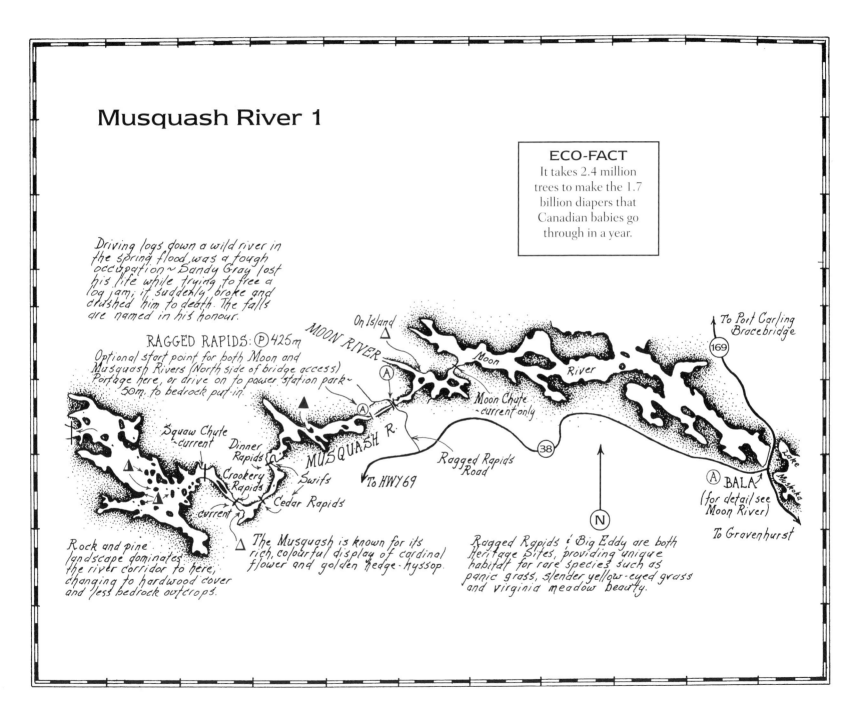

Driving logs down a wild river in the spring flood, was a tough occupation ~ Sandy Gray lost his life while trying to free a log jam; it suddenly broke and crushed him to death. The falls are named in his honour.

RAGGED RAPIDS: Ⓟ 425m
Optional start point for both Moon and Musquash Rivers (North side of bridge access) Portage here, or drive on to pauer station park ~ 50m. to bedrock put-in.

MOON RIVER

On Island △

To Port Carling Bracebridge

169

Moon River

Moon Chute ~ current only

MUSQUASH R.

Squaw Chute ~ current

Dinner Rapids

Crookery Rapids

Swifs

Cedar Rapids

current

38

Ragged Rapids Road

To HWY 69

Ⓐ BALA
(for detail see Moon River)

To Gravenhurst

Lake Muskoka

Rock and pine landscape dominates the river corridor to here, changing to hardwood cover and less bedrock outcrops.

△ The Musquash is known for its rich, colourful display of cardinal flower and golden hedge-hyssop.

N

Ragged Rapids & Big Eddy are both Heritage Sites, providing unique habitat for rare species such as panic grass, slender yellow-eyed grass and virginia meadow beauty.

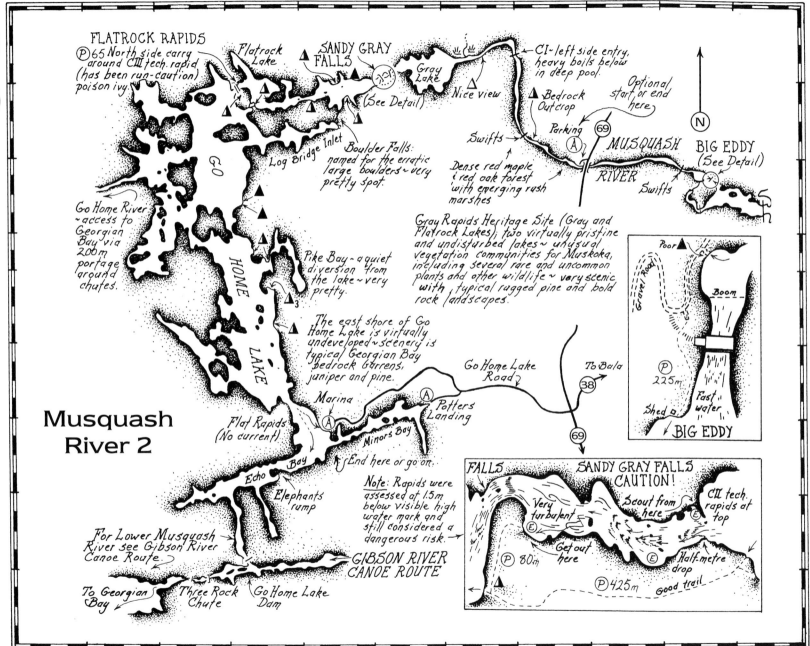

SEGUIN RIVER
Sigwan zibbi SPRING RIVER

The Seguin River is separated into two sections for easy reference: (A) Isabel Lake to Hurdville Road bridge, and (B) Hurdville Road bridge to Parry Sound.

CLASSIFICATION (A) intermediate, (B) experienced novice (if Seguin/Mountain Chutes portaged)

DISTANCE (A) 12.2 km, (B) 14.5 km

TIME (A) 1 day, (B) 1 day

SEASON (A) mid-April to mid-July, (B) mid April through October

ELEVATION DROP (A) 15 m, (B) 29 m

CAMPSITES (A) 5, (B) 2

RAPIDS & FALLS (including Mountain Chutes) 13 CIs, 5 CIIs, 1 CIII

PORTAGES (A) 2 (700 m), can be shortened to one 300 m carry; (B) 3 (1010 m), can be shortened to 285 m if Mountain Chutes is run

MAPS 31 E/5, 41 H/8 & H/7 (one map)

ACCESS (A) Highway 518 North on Isabel Lake Road, 4 km to Seguin River bridge; (B) Hurdville Road north to Seguin River bridge

TAKE-OUT (A) Hurdville Road bridge, (B) Bobby Orr Community Centre in Parry Sound

SPECIALIZED GEAR wetsuits for spring runs, ABS canoes for (A)

WHITEWATER CHARACTERISTICS & GENERAL HAZARDS There is always that temptation to run the more difficult rapids. Seguin Canyon during high water flow can be quite dangerous. Use caution, take your lumps on the portage, and revel in the grand view from the bottom in dry clothes. Once the water level retreats, it leaves behind boulder fields and gravel shallows, which will require more wading, lining and portaging. On approach to Parry Sound, Mill Lake can get quite rough past Robinson's Point. If the wind is too strong from the south or west, it is better to take out at the bridge where the Seguin turns south past Mountain Basin Lake.

ECOLOGY The newly designated Seguin Conservation Reserve (324 ha) protects upland forests of poplar, red oak, sugar maple and stately white pine. Located along the section of river above and including Mountain Chutes and below, the typical steep cliff habitats are home for the turkey vulture.

FEATURES "That brings to mind the lads…whose lives in seasons past were the price of Seguin Pine." Parry Sound's legendary logger, Seguin Sam, may have hummed a few bars of this traditional ditty as he danced a jig on the cut pine that filled the river each spring on the way to the sawmill. You can still see remains of the cut logs poking up from the river bottom, some partly floating as deadheads and others lying scattered beyond the banks. Every year the Seguin Canoe Club initiates the paddling season here. I can't say enough about this stellar river; the whitewater play is exceptional and the scenery breathtaking. The upper river is strictly for the whitewater enthusiast, but my favourite run, without question, is Mountain Chutes, with its decadent boulder riffs and swirling eddies. The lower course is through Georgian Bay coastal landscape, rugged and bold, and offers the novice paddler a superior river and lake outing.

Seguin River 1

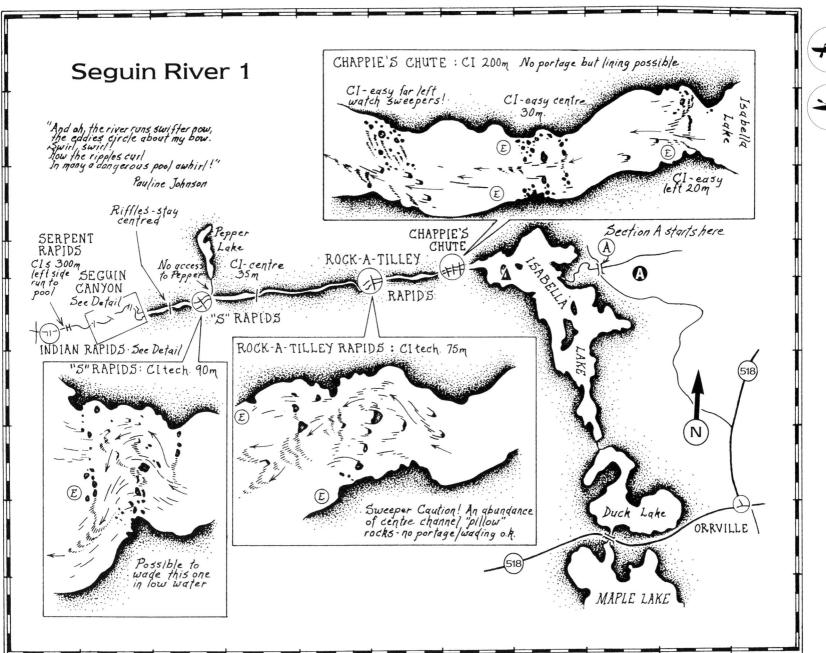

"And oh, the river runs swifter now,
the eddies circle about my bow.
Swirl, swirl!
How the ripples curl
In many a dangerous pool awhirl!"

Pauline Johnson

CHAPPIE'S CHUTE : CI 200m *No portage but lining possible*

CI-easy far left
watch sweepers!

CI-easy centre
30m

(E)

(E)

CI-easy
left 20m

(E)

Isabella Lake

SERPENT RAPIDS

CI s 300m
left side
run to pool

Riffles - stay centred

Pepper Lake

No access to Pepper

CI-centre 35m

ROCK-A-TILLEY

CHAPPIE'S CHUTE

Section A starts here

(A)

A

SEGUIN CANYON
See Detail

"S" RAPIDS

RAPIDS

(triangle)

ISABELLA LAKE

(-71-)

INDIAN RAPIDS *See Detail*

"S" RAPIDS : CI tech. 90m

(E)

(E)

Possible to
wade this one
in low water

ROCK-A-TILLEY RAPIDS : CI tech. 75m

(E)

(E)

Sweeper Caution! An abundance
of centre channel "pillow"
rocks - no portage/wading o.k.

N

(518)

(1)

Duck Lake

ORRVILLE

(518)

MAPLE LAKE

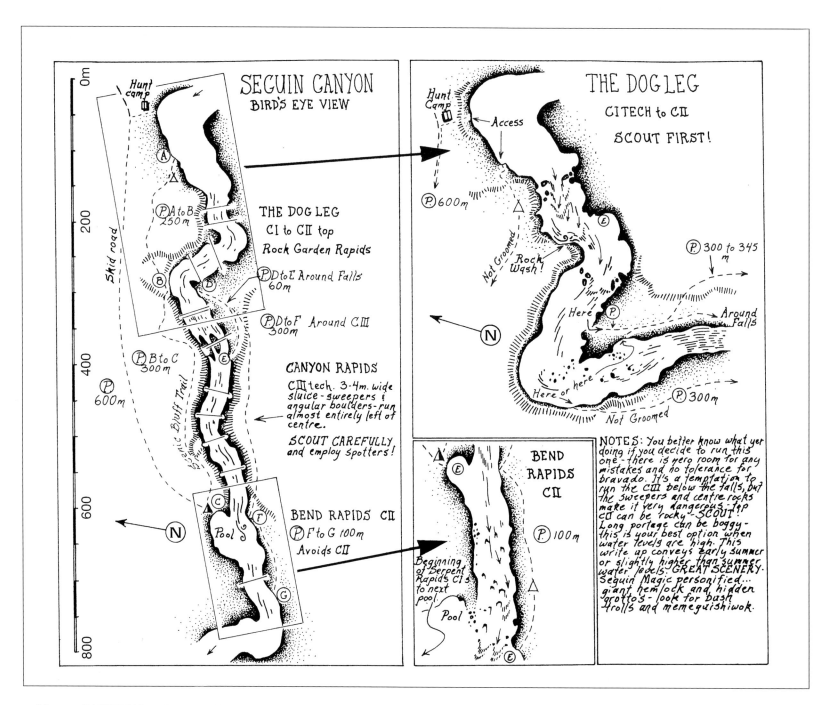

SEGUIN CANYON
BIRD'S EYE VIEW

Hunt camp

0m

Skid road

Ⓐ

Ⓟ A to B
250m

THE DOG LEG
CI to CII top
Rock Garden Rapids

200

Ⓑ

Ⓑ

Ⓟ D to E Around Falls
60m

Ⓟ D to F Around CIII
300m

Ⓟ B to C
300m

Scenic Bluff Trail

400

Ⓔ

CANYON RAPIDS

CIII tech. 3-4 m. wide
sluice-sweepers &
angular boulders-run
almost entirely left of
centre.

SCOUT CAREFULLY
and employ spotters!

Ⓟ
600m

600

Ⓒ

Ⓕ

Pool

Ⓝ

BEND RAPIDS CII

Ⓟ F to G 100m

Avoids CII

Ⓖ

800

THE DOG LEG
CI TECH to CII
SCOUT FIRST!

Hunt Camp

Access

Ⓟ 600m

Rock Wash!

Not Groomed

Ⓔ

Ⓟ 300 to 345 m

Here

Ⓟ

Here or here

Not Groomed

Around Falls

Ⓟ 300m

Ⓝ

Δ
Ⓔ

BEND RAPIDS
CII

Ⓟ 100m

Beginning
of Serpent
Rapids CIs
to next
pool.

Pool

Δ

Ⓔ

NOTES: You better know what yer
doing if you decide to run this
one - there is nero room for any
mistakes and no tolerance for
bravado. It's a temptation to
run the CIII below the falls, but
the sweepers and centre rocks
make it very dangerous. Top
CII can be rocky - SCOUT!
Long portage can be boggy -
this is your best option when
water levels are high. This
write up conveys early summer
or slightly higher than summer
water levels. GREAT SCENERY.
Seguin Magic personified...
giant hemlock and hidden
grottos - look for bush
trolls and memeguishiwok.

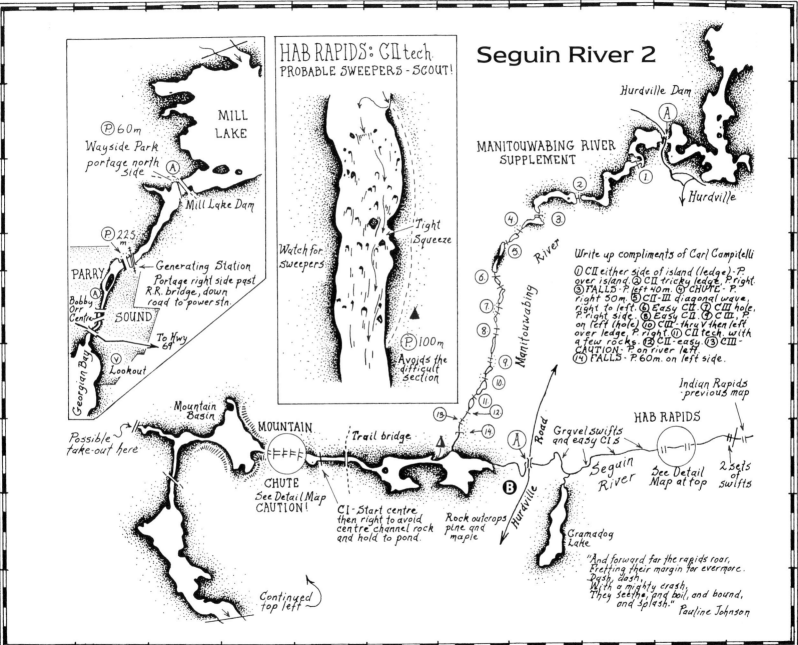

Seguin River 2

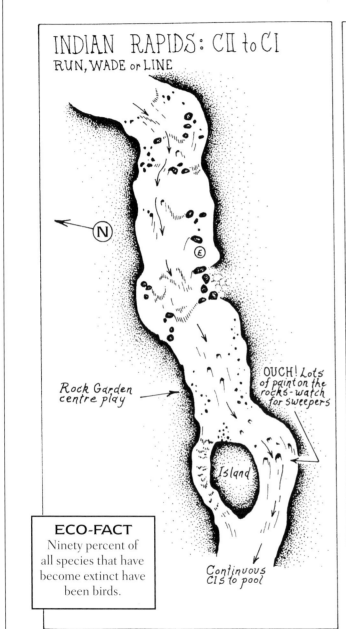

INDIAN RAPIDS: CII to CI
RUN, WADE or LINE

N

Rock Garden
centre play

OUCH! Lots
of paint on the
rocks - watch
for sweepers

Island

Continuous
CIS to pool

ECO-FACT
Ninety percent of
all species that have
become extinct have
been birds.

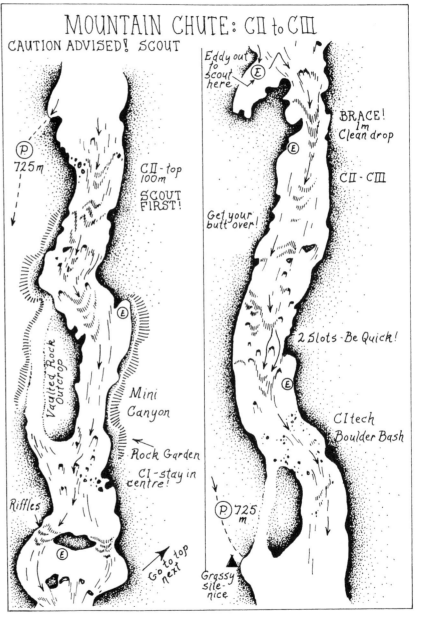

MOUNTAIN CHUTE: CII to CIII
CAUTION ADVISED! SCOUT

Eddy out
to scout
here

P
725m

CII - top
100m

SCOUT
FIRST!

Vaulted Rock
Outcrop

Mini
Canyon

Rock Garden
CI - stay in
centre!

Riffles

Go to top
next

BRACE!
1m
Clean drop

CII - CIII

Get your
butt over!

2 Slots - Be Quick!

CI tech
Boulder Bash

P 725 m

Grassy
site -
nice

SEVERN RIVER
The Rocklands

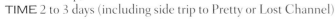

CLASSIFICATION novice; Lost Channel Loop, experienced novice if rapids are portaged

DISTANCE Highway 11 at Severn Bridge to Port Severn, 54 km; Lost Channel Loop, 14 km

TIME 2 to 3 days (including side trip to Pretty or Lost Channel)

SEASON May through October

ELEVATION DROP 34 m

CAMPSITES There are several privately run camping areas along the route and a selection of lodges and camps, generally located at the major stopover points.

PORTAGES 2 (335 m)

MAPS 31 D/14, 31 D/13

ACCESS either Severn River bridge or Shamrock Marina (3 km west off Highway 11)

TAKE-OUT Port Severn or Big Chute

SPECIALIZED GEAR none

WHITEWATER CHARACTERISTICS & GENERAL HAZARDS Unless you plan on paddling downstream along Pretty Channel, there is no whitewater on this route except for some sections of current through the narrow cuts. Pretty Channel is a difficult, advanced class run, and novices should not attempt whitewater along this stretch. However, there are good portage trails that bypass all of the rapids. Hazards along the Severn River include danger from high winds on Sparrow and Gloucester Pool; boat wake, particularly on the weekends; and undertows and boils at the outflow of dams.

ECOLOGY The Severn topography is dominated by undulating gneissic bedrock ridges with ravine basins containing sandy till deposits and wetland pockets. This is an outstanding habitat for several rare flora and fauna species, including wild garlic, spotted St. John's wort, Virginia mountain mint, fragrant sumac, eastern hognose snake, spotted turtle, red-shouldered hawk and Massasauga rattlesnake. Prairie species include big bluestem, cord grass, prairie dropseed, Indian grass and switch grass.

FEATURES As a novice class route, specifically for touring kayakers, this is an exceptional trip. The Severn marks the beginning of the Precambrian Shield mantle in all its glory. The gneissic "rocklands," even though part of the busy Trent-Severn recreational waterway, still retain a remote and extremely beautiful character. As a result of calcareous (limestone-inundated) waters flowing over the edge of the Shield from the south, the river contains an extraordinary diversity of aquatic plants — among the richest in Canada.

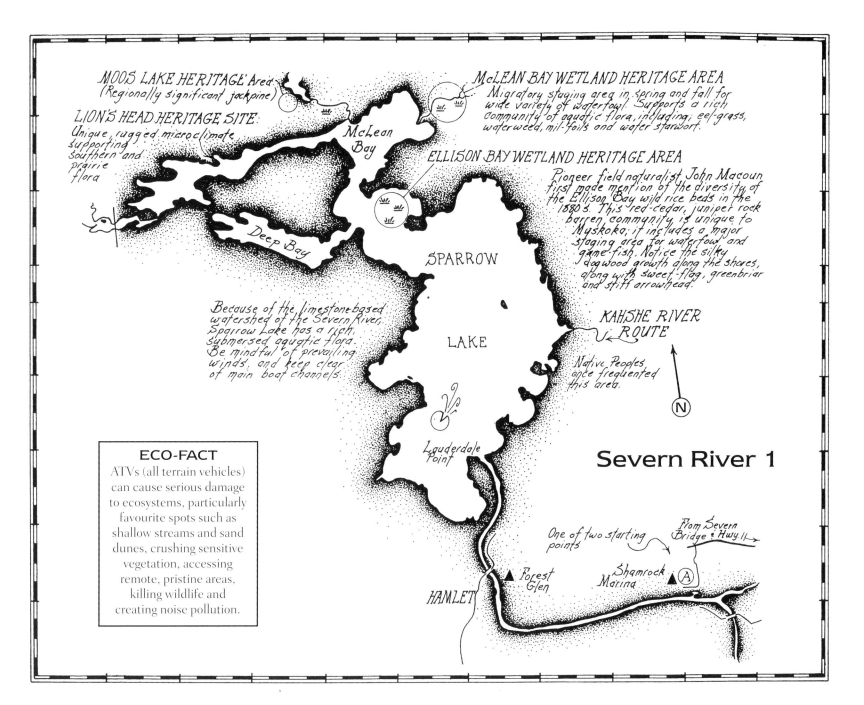

MOOS LAKE HERITAGE Area (Regionally significant jackpine)

LION'S HEAD HERITAGE SITE: Unique, rugged microclimate supporting southern and prairie flora

McLEAN BAY WETLAND HERITAGE AREA Migratory staging area in spring and fall for wide variety of waterfowl. Supports a rich community of aquatic flora, including: eel-grass, waterweed, mil-foils and water starwort.

McLean Bay

Deep Bay

ELLISON BAY WETLAND HERITAGE AREA Pioneer field naturalist John Macoun first made mention of the diversity of the Ellison Bay wild rice beds in the 1880's. This red-cedar, juniper rock barren, community is unique to Muskoka; it includes a major staging area for waterfowl and game fish. Notice the silky dogwood growth along the shores, along with sweet-flag, greenbriar and stiff arrowhead.

SPARROW

LAKE

Because of the limestone-based watershed of the Severn River, Sparrow Lake has a rich, submersed aquatic flora. Be mindful of prevailing winds, and keep clear of main boat channels.

KAHSHE RIVER ROUTE

Native Peoples once frequented this area.

N

Lauderdale Point

Severn River 1

ECO-FACT
ATVs (all terrain vehicles) can cause serious damage to ecosystems, particularly favourite spots such as shallow streams and sand dunes, crushing sensitive vegetation, accessing remote, pristine areas, killing wildlife and creating noise pollution.

One of two starting points

From Severn Bridge & Hwy. 11

Shamrock Marina

A

HAMLET

Forest Glen

Severn River 2

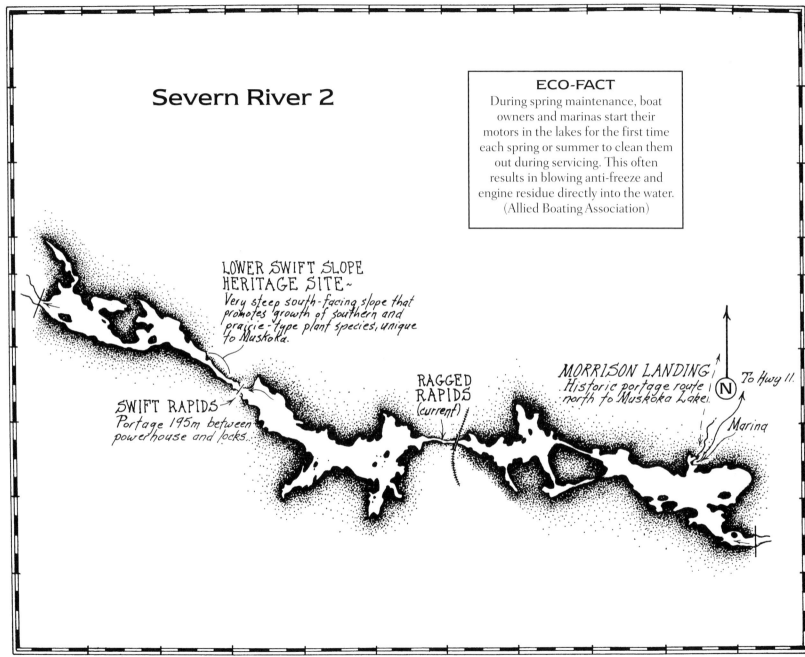

LOWER SWIFT SLOPE HERITAGE SITE ~
Very steep south-facing slope that promotes growth of southern and prairie-type plant species, unique to Muskoka.

SWIFT RAPIDS
Portage 195m between powerhouse and locks.

RAGGED RAPIDS
(current)

MORRISON LANDING
Historic portage route north to Muskoka Lake.

To Hwy 11.

N

Marina

Severn River 3

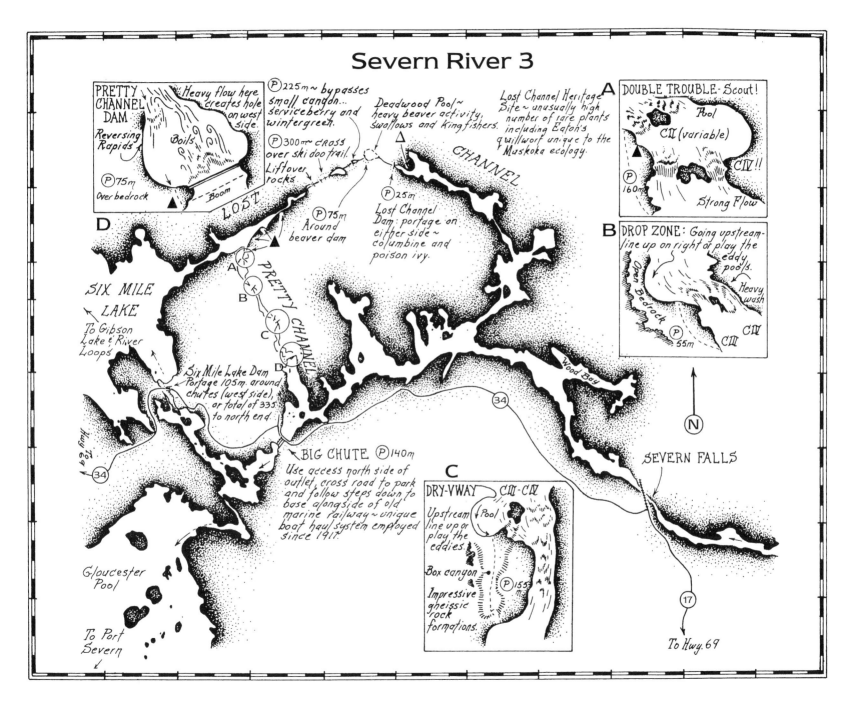

PRETTY CHANNEL DAM

Heavy flow here creates hole on west side.

Reversing Rapids

Boils

Ⓟ 75m Over bedrock

Boom

D

LOST

Ⓟ 225m ~ bypasses small canyon... serviceberry and wintergreen.

Ⓟ 300m ~ cross over skidoo trail.

Liftover rocks

Deadwood Pool ~ heavy beaver activity, swallows and Kingfishers.

Lost Channel Heritage Site ~ unusually high number of rare plants including Eaton's quillwort unique to the Muskoka ecology.

CHANNEL

Ⓟ 25m

Lost Channel Dam: portage on either side ~ columbine and poison ivy.

Ⓟ 75m Around beaver dam

A

DOUBLE TROUBLE ~ Scout!

Pool CIII (variable)

Ⓟ 160m

CIV !!

Strong Flow

B

DROP ZONE: Going upstream ~ line up on right or play the eddy pool/s.

Open Bedrock

Heavy wash

Ⓟ 55m

CIII

SIX MILE LAKE

To Gibson Lake & River Loops

D

A Ⓡ

B Ⓡ

C Ⓡ

D Ⓡ

PRETTY CHANNEL

Six Mile Lake Dam Portage 105m. around chutes (west side), or total of 335 to north end.

Wood Bay

34

N

SEVERN FALLS

Hwy 69

34

BIG CHUTE Ⓟ 140m

Use access north side of outlet, cross road to park and follow steps down to base alongside of old marine railway ~ unique boat haul system employed since 1917.

C

DRY-VWAY CIII - CIV

Upstream line up or play the eddies.

Pool

Box canyon

Ⓟ 155m

Impressive gneissic rock formations.

Gloucester Pool

To Port Severn

17

To Hwy. 69

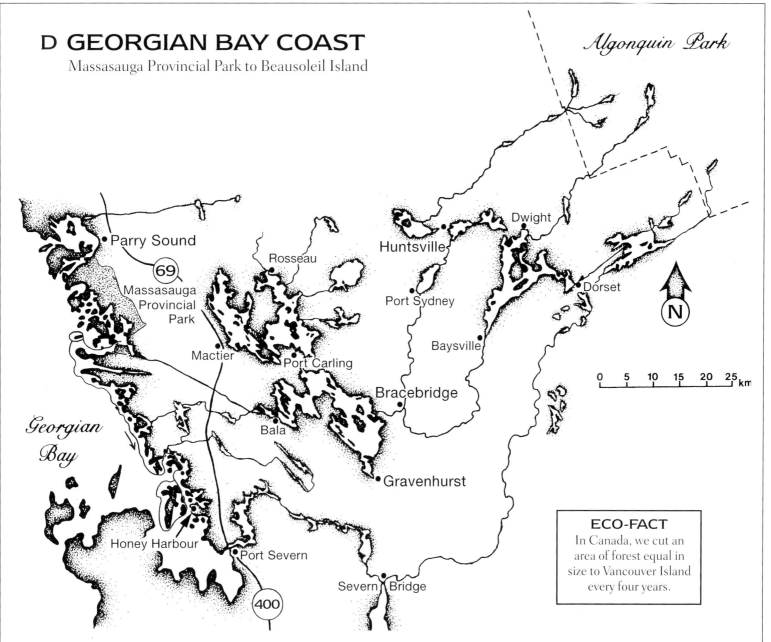

D GEORGIAN BAY COAST
Massasauga Provincial Park to Beausoleil Island

Algonquin Park

Parry Sound

69

Massasauga
Provincial
Park

Rosseau

Huntsville

Dwight

Port Sydney

Dorset

N

Baysville

Mactier

Port Carling

Bracebridge

Georgian

Bay

Bala

0 5 10 15 20 25 km

Gravenhurst

Honey Harbour

Port Severn

400

Severn Bridge

ECO-FACT
In Canada, we cut an
area of forest equal in
size to Vancouver Island
every four years.

GEORGIAN BAY COAST
The Heritage Coast
Massasauga Provincial Park to Beausoleil Island

CLASSIFICATION novice (avoiding any expanse of water, summer trips only); experienced novice (off-season travel and some open-water crossings that may become rough)

DISTANCE Pete's Place access to Honey Harbour via Wreck Island Loop, Moreaus Bay, Long Island, Freddy Channel, Bone Island, McCrae Lake chutes, Deer Island channel — 83 km; Pine Island tour, add 13 km; Beausoleil Island tour, add 19.5 km

TIME 6 to 8 days

SEASON June through September (optimum conditions)

CAMPSITES 42 established sites en route in Massasauga Park; 4 to 6 along the coast with several undesignated sites; 6 along the northeast shore of Beausoleil Island (busy in summer)

MAPS & CHARTS 31 E/4, 31 D/13, 41 H/1 (Marine Chart 2202)

ACCESS Pete's Place in Massasauga Provincial Park

TAKE-OUT Honey Harbour; options are Moose Point or McDonald Lake at Highway 69 (2 short portages)

FEE Massasauga Provincial Park overnight camping fee and Georgian Bay National Park island use fees

ADDITIONAL RESOURCES Massasauga Park map; *Kayaking Georgian Bay* by Jonathan Reynolds and Heather Smith; *A Paddler's Guide to Ontario's Cottage Country* by Kevin Callan

SPECIALIZED GEAR appropriate touring kayaks equipped with safety equipment (throwbag, bilge pump, paddle-float bag, whistle); either skeg or rudder system recommended for steering

GENERAL HAZARDS & CONSIDERATIONS Open-water paddling and sudden coastal storms may produce dangerous conditions for travelling. Be wary of weather changes — electrical and wind storms come in quickly. Georgian Bay is home to the Eastern Massasauga rattlesnake and is prime habitat for poison ivy. Be careful when walking through dense undergrowth or collecting firewood, and keep your pets leashed and children in sight. Boat wake on main channels can be annoying and dangerous during peak times, especially weekends, so it is best to avoid this congested period if possible, or keep out of the centre, buoyed zones where motorcraft frequent. Please be considerate of private property and the sensitive coastal environment.

ECOLOGY Call it a Heritage Coast or even a Littoral Biosphere Reserve, the Georgian Bay Coast is one of the most celebrated ecological wonders of Ontario. Starting in Massasauga Natural Environment Park, you'll find Muskoka's only colony of black-crowned night herons; a trek around Wreck Island may offer a chance encounter with a rattlesnake and a good look at a unique geological phenomenon. Georgian Bay Islands National Park system, Bone and Beausoleil Islands all offer unique habitats and natural adventures. There are too many ecological features to describe here. Seek out the available literature before heading to the coast, which boasts of one of the richest and most diverse flora and fauna habitats in Canada. No camping on Pine Islands, thank you!

FEATURES "You can throw away time, just for the pleasure of wasting it…on Georgian Bay," are lines from a song by Connie Calder. There's definitely something about Georgian Bay that makes time, job and responsibilities seem immaterial. Coastal paddling does glorify the eternal mix of earth, sky and water. This portion of Muskoka coast, with its deep bays, inlets and channels, offers the touring kayaker numerous trip options and side treks, including Wreck and Pine Islands. The remarkable and tenacious landscape has inspired the Group of Seven artists, poets and songwriters.

FOR MORE INFORMATION

Massasauga Park: For reservations call 705-378-2401. For maps write to RR 2 Parry Sound, Ontario P2A 2W8. Familiarize yourself with park regulations and costs.

Georgian Bay Islands National Park: For maps and fee schedule call 705-756-2415. Write Box 28, Honey Harbour, Ontario P0E 1E0. Website http://parkscanada.pch.gc.ca

VHF Marine Radio: Channel 16, Park Warden & Canadian Coast Guard Rescue Unit

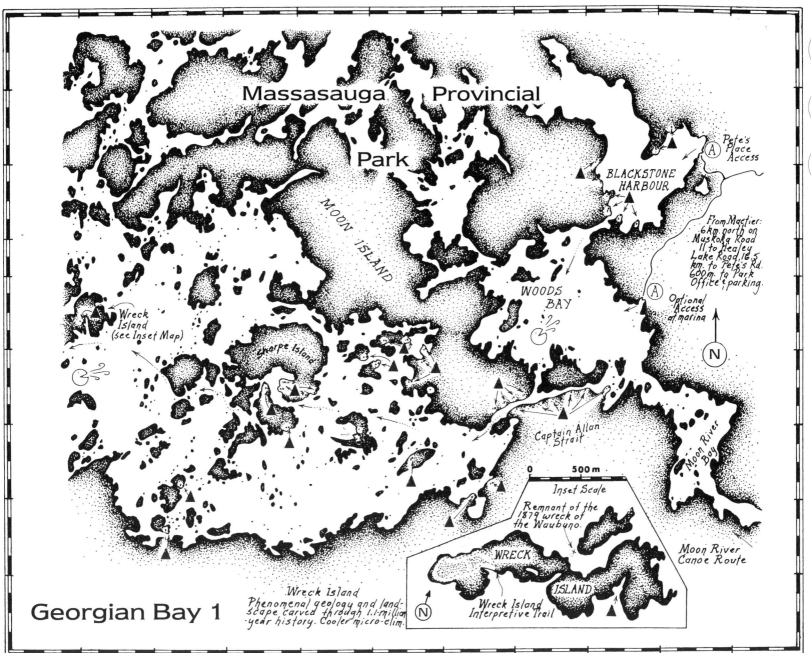

Massasauga Provincial Park

MOON ISLAND

WOODS BAY

Pete's Place Access

BLACKSTONE HARBOUR

From Maetier: 6km north on Muskoka Road 11 to Healey Lake Road, 16.5 km. to Pete's Rd. 600m. to Park Office & parking.

Ⓐ Optional Access at marina

N

Wreck Island (see Inset Map)

Sharpe Island

Captain Allan Strait

Moon River Bay

Moon River Canoe Route

Georgian Bay 1

Wreck Island
Phenomenal geology and landscape carved through 1.1 million year history. Cooler micro-clim.

0   500 m
Inset Scale

Remnant of the 1879 wreck of the Waubuno.

WRECK ISLAND

Wreck Island Interpretive Trail

N

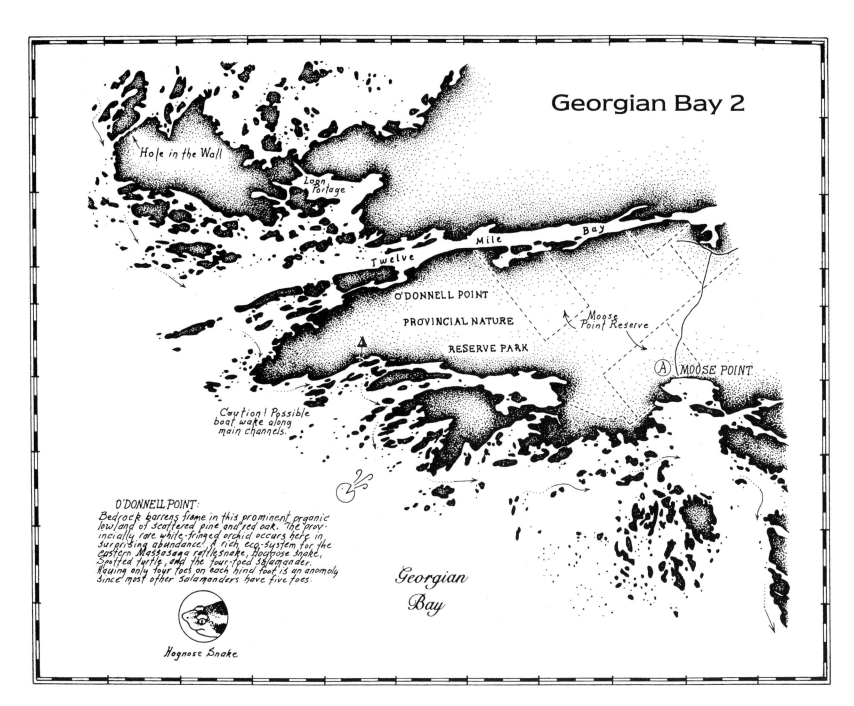

Georgian Bay 2

Hole in the Wall

Loon Portage

Twelve Mile Bay

O'DONNELL POINT

PROVINCIAL NATURE

RESERVE PARK

Moose Point Reserve

Ⓐ MOOSE POINT

Caution! Possible boat wake along main channels.

O'DONNELL POINT:
Bedrock barrens frame in this prominent organic lowland of scattered pine and red oak. The provincially rare white-fringed orchid occurs here in surprising abundance. A rich eco-system for the eastern Massasaga rattlesnake, Hognose snake, Spotted turtle, and the four-toed salamander. Having only four toes on each hind foot is an anomaly since most other salamanders have five toes.

Hognose Snake

Georgian Bay

Georgian Bay 3

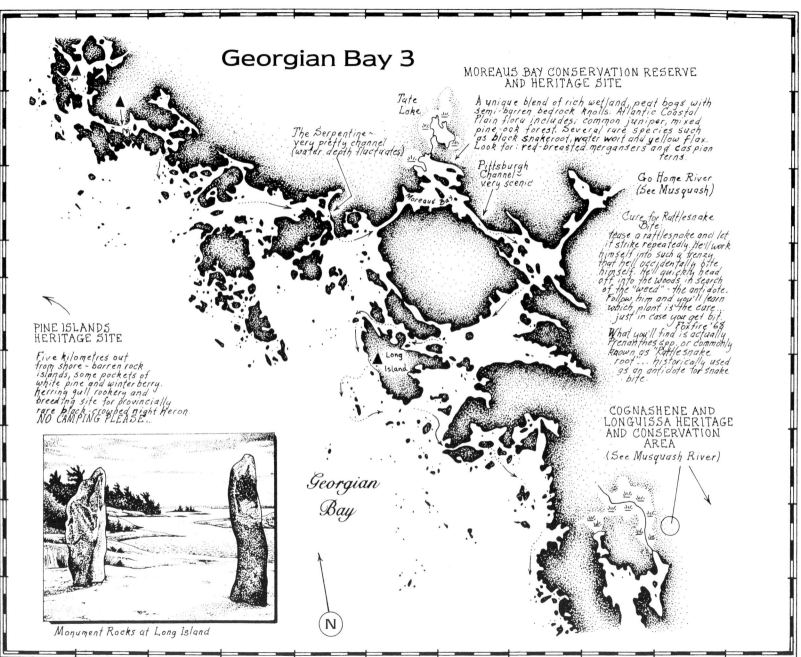

MOREAUS BAY CONSERVATION RESERVE
AND HERITAGE SITE

A unique blend of rich wetland, peat bogs with
semi-barren bedrock knolls. Atlantic Coastal
Plain flora includes: common juniper, mixed
pine-oak forest. Several rare species such
as black snakeroot, water wort and yellow flax.
Look for: red-breasted mergansers and caspian
terns.

Tate Lake

The Serpentine~
very pretty channel
(water depth fluctuates)

Pittsburgh
Channel~
very scenic

Moreaus Bay

Go Home River
(See Musquash)

Cure for Rattlesnake
Bite:
tease a rattlesnake and let
it strike repeatedly. He'll work
himself into such a frenzy
that he'll accidentally bite
himself. He'll quickly head
off into the woods in search
of the "weed" ~ the antidote.
Follow him and you'll learn
which plant is the cure...
just in case you get bit.
Foxfire '68
What you'll find is actually
Trenanthes sep, or commonly
known as "Rattlesnake
root"... historically used
as an antidote for snake
bite.

PINE ISLANDS
HERITAGE SITE

Five kilometres out
from shore ~ barren rock
islands, some pockets of
white pine and winterberry.
herring gull rookery and
breeding site for provincially
rare black-crowned night heron.
NO CAMPING PLEASE...

Long Island

COGNASHENE AND
LONGUISSA HERITAGE
AND CONSERVATION
AREA

(See Musquash River)

Georgian Bay

N

Monument Rocks at Long Island

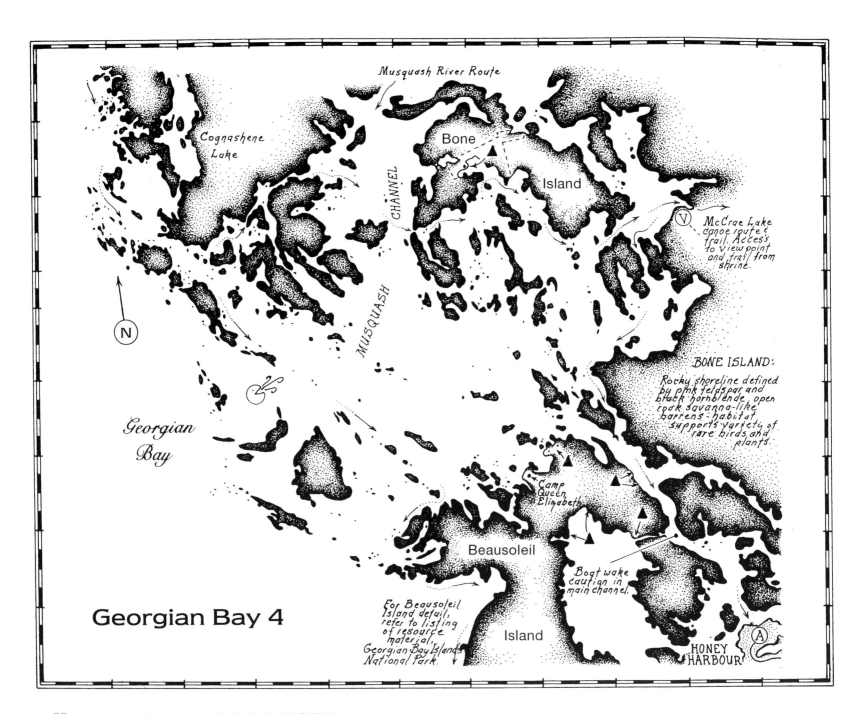

Musquash River Route

Cognashene
Lake

Bone

Island

CHANNEL

MUSQUASH

N

Georgian

Bay

(V) McCrae Lake
canoe route &
trail. Access
to view point
and trail from
shrine.

BONE ISLAND:
Rocky shoreline defined
by pink feldspar and
black hornblende, open
rock savanna-like
barrens - habitat
supports variety of
rare birds and
plants.

Camp
Queen
Elizabeth

Beausoleil

Boat wake
caution in
main channel.

Georgian Bay 4

For Beausoleil
Island detail,
refer to listing
of resource
material,
Georgian Bay Islands
National Park.

Island

(A)

HONEY
HARBOUR

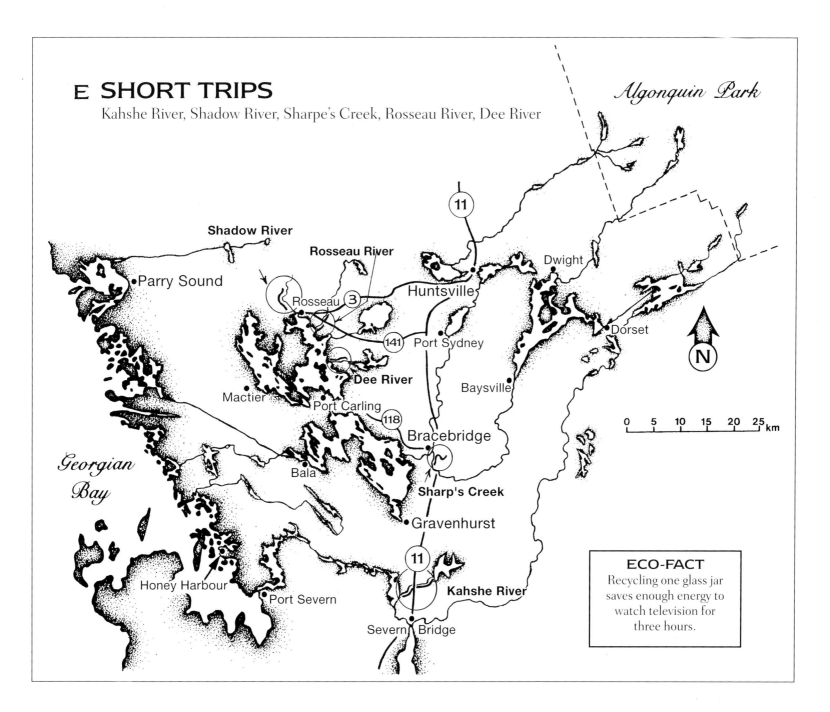

E SHORT TRIPS

Kahshe River, Shadow River, Sharpe's Creek, Rosseau River, Dee River

Algonquin Park

Shadow River

Rosseau River

⑪

Dwight

• Parry Sound

Rosseau ③

Huntsville

Georgian Bay

⑭1 Port Sydney

Dorset

N

Dee River

Baysville

Mactier •

Port Carling

⑪8

Bala

Bracebridge

0 5 10 15 20 25 km

Sharp's Creek

• Gravenhurst

Honey Harbour

⑪

Port Severn •

Kahshe River

ECO-FACT
Recycling one glass jar saves enough energy to watch television for three hours.

Severn Bridge

KAHSHE RIVER
MUSKOKA'S HEARTLAND GEM

CLASSIFICATION Experienced novice paddlers must take out at the Kahshe River Campgrounds and continue the trip at the picnic area on the west side of Highway 11, otherwise this is considered a spring intermediate course.

DISTANCE Kahshe Lake to Sparrow Lake (Lauderdale Point Marina), 13 km; or 9 km to Muskoka Road 13 bridge

TIME 1 day

SEASON as early as late March for spring runs, until late June through October west of Highway 11

ELEVATION DROP 33 m

PORTAGES 5 (730 m); can be shortened to 415 m by creative running and lining

CAMPSITES 2 private campgrounds (Hillbilly, Kahshe River)

RAPIDS & FALLS 7 (2 CIs, 2CIIs, 1 CIII, 2 waterfalls)

MAP 31 D/14

ACCESS South Kahshe Lake Road off Highway 11 to dam, or Highway 11 picnic area for novice jaunts

TAKE-OUT Kahshe River Campgrounds (novice, at Highway 11 bypass) to Muskoka Road 13 (early spring take-out if ice is still on Sparrow); or Lauderdale Point Marina off Muskoka Road 49 via Muskoka Road 13

SPECIALIZED GEAR cold-weather gear and wetsuits for spring runs

WHITEWATER CHARACTERISTICS & GENERAL HAZARDS The most difficult stretch lies between the Kahshe River Campgrounds and Highway 11. The sluice under Highway 11 cannot be scouted or portaged in the early season and there may be blockages to consider. Approach with caution. Wading is possible here during low water. Rapids become very rocky with pronounced ledge drops when the water level is low. Other considerations are ice conditions on Sparrow Lake for safe take-out, and prevailing winds. Check weather and ice-out conditions ahead of time.

ECOLOGY Within ten minutes of putting in at the Kahshe Dam, I spotted a deer only metres away; it bounded from the shore thicket, stopped abruptly to observe my presence, and then sauntered off seemingly undisturbed by my passing. The drumming of ruffed grouse kept up a steady beat along the entire river. For naturalists, the lower river, below Highway 11, is a veritable Garden of Eden, particularly adjacent to Clipsham's Wood, where a warmer microclimate supports flora and fauna of a more southern affinity. There is a definite transition from the typical pine and rock Shield landscape of the upper river to a more pastoral setting. You'll see a wide variety of ducks feeding in the shallow bays and a number of shoreline birds such as kingfishers, swallows and great blue herons. Artefacts found here attest to prehistoric human use of the river mouth, and Sparrow Lake is home to Muskoka's only petroglyph site.

FEATURES For those whitewater enthusiasts too impatient to wait until decent weather, the Kahshe is a perfect primer for the paddling season, or just a pleasant spring jaunt on a sunny afternoon. I've been on the river as early as March 6 while the Kahshe was at its peak and the winter ice was only just beginning to melt away from the lake shorelines. You'll want to pick a day when snow is not in the forecast.

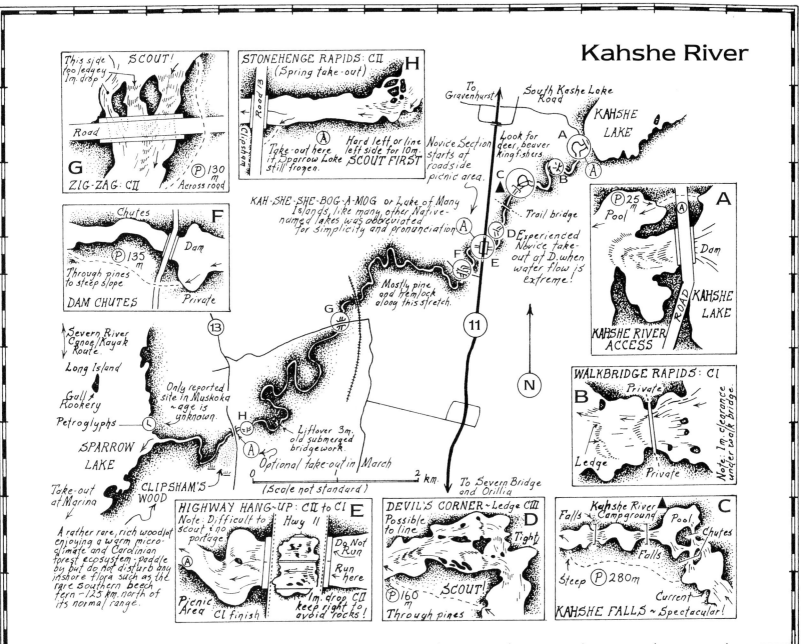

SHADOW RIVER
POETRY IN MOTION

CLASSIFICATION experienced novice (from top end), novice below Highway 141

DISTANCE 9 km (4.6 km from the Highway 141 bridge)

TIME upper river start, full-day paddle, 5 to 7 hours; lower river tour, 2 to 3 hours

SEASON upper river, April to May; lower river, April through October

ELEVATION DROP 40 m

PORTAGES upper river only, 4 (515 m); longest carry is 240 m

CAMPSITES none

RAPIDS & FALLS 4 sections of chutes and falls, occasional riffles and gentle current

MAP 31 E/5

ACCESS Highway 141 to Nipissing Road north 3.5 km to side road and bridge over river. Lower river access from Highway 141 bridge or paddle upstream from town of Rosseau

TAKE-OUT Rosseau marina or beach park

SPECIALIZED GEAR picnic basket, sunscreen and book of Pauline Johnson poetry

WHITEWATER CHARACTERISTICS & GENERAL HAZARDS During peak flow there is some strong current and the possibility of "sweepers" (trees across current). At the time of writing, none of the portages had been maintained but were passable. Please respect all private land and backcountry ethics.

ECOLOGY This is predominantly a wetland ecosystem, broken occasionally by bands of open bedrock. Look for beaver activity, great blue heron, osprey, several species of ducks, muskrat and deer. Mostly second-growth hemlock and pine with a generous ground cover of wintergreen, serviceberry and fern deck the upper river landscape, while maple and oak canopy the lower course.

FEATURES I left my bicycle at the Rosseau marina and drove the 6.1 km to the starting point. It was April and the Shadow, or White Oak Creek, as it was once called, was running high. At peak flow the river was barely a canoe-length wide but sufficiently deep enough to float my boat. I was intrigued by the numerous testimonials of turn-of-the-century tourists and celebrities. Here was a river whose reflections of the overhanging oak conveyed a mystical aura — a "weightlessness" of such notoriety that I had to explore this phenomenon for myself. I was not disappointed. It was obvious that few people had travelled the upper river in quite some time. And if the lower river commanded such exultation, the upper course was even more a revelation of treasure to the senses. For the more adventurous, the upper 3 km provide a congenial mix of meandering creek wetland and Precambrian rock outcrops, with some of Muskoka's quaintest chutes and cascades. The lower section can be paddled up or downstream without difficulty and, as Pauline Johnson exclaims, you'll find yourself floating as "a bubble in the pearly air…midway 'twixt earth and heaven."

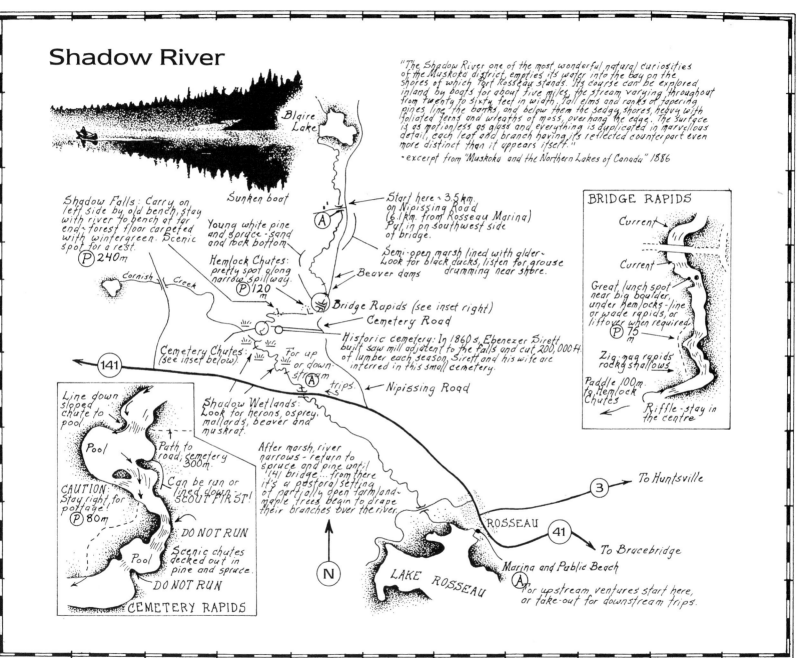

Shadow River

"The Shadow River one of the most wonderful natural curiosities of the Muskoka district, empties its water into the bay on the shores of which Port Rosseau stands. Its course can be explored inland by boats for about five miles, the stream varying throughout from twenty to sixty feet in width. Tall elms and ranks of tapering pines line the banks, and below them the sedgy shores, heavy with foliated ferns and wreaths of moss, overhang the edge. The surface is as motionless as glass and everything is duplicated in marvellous detail, each leaf and branch having its reflected counterpart even more distinct than it appears itself."

- excerpt from "Muskoka and the Northern Lakes of Canada" 1886

Blaire Lake

Sunken boat

Start here - 3.5 km. on Nipissing Road (6.1 km. from Rosseau Marina) Put in on southwest side of bridge.

(A)

Semi-open marsh lined with alder - Look for black ducks, listen for grouse drumming near shore.

Beaver dams

Shadow Falls: Carry on left side by old bench, stay with river to bench at far end - forest floor carpeted with wintergreen. Scenic spot for a rest.
(P) 240 m

Young white pine and spruce - sand and rock bottom.

Hemlock Chutes: pretty spot along narrow spillway.
(P) 120 m

Cornish Creek

Bridge Rapids (see inset right)

Cemetery Road

Historic cemetery: In 1860's, Ebenezer Sirett built saw mill adjacent to the falls and cut 200,000 ft. of lumber each season. Sirett and his wife are interred in this small cemetery.

Cemetery Chutes: (see inset below).

For up or down-stream trips.

(A)

(141)

Nipissing Road

Shadow Wetlands: Look for herons, osprey, mallards, beaver and muskrat.

After marsh, river narrows - return to spruce and pine until 141 bridge... from there it's a pastoral setting of partially open farmland - maple trees begin to drape their branches over the river.

(3) → To Huntsville

ROSSEAU

(41) → To Bracebridge

Marina and Public Beach
(A) For upstream ventures start here, or take-out for downstream trips.

LAKE ROSSEAU

N

BRIDGE RAPIDS

Current

Current

Great lunch spot near big boulder, under hemlocks - line or wade rapids, or liftover when required.
(P) 75 m

Zig-zag rapids rocky shallows

Paddle 100 m. to Hemlock Chutes

Riffle - stay in the centre

CEMETERY RAPIDS

Line down sloped chute to pool

Pool

Path to road, cemetery 300 m.

CAUTION: Stay right for portage!
(P) 80 m

Can be run or lined down - SCOUT FIRST!

DO NOT RUN

Scenic chutes decked out in pine and spruce.

Pool

DO NOT RUN

SHARPE'S CREEK

Including South Muskoka River Canyon

CLASSIFICATION novice

DISTANCE Bracebridge to South Falls and return, including Sharpe's Creek, 16.5 km

TIME allow 4 to 6 hours

SEASON May through October

PORTAGES none

CAMPSITES Bracebridge Park and Annie Williams Park (several B & Bs nearby)

RAPIDS & FALLS Bracebridge and South Falls and Sharpe's Creek Cascades (some current and swifts during high flow periods in spring and after heavy rainfall)

MAP 31 E/3

ACCESS & TAKE-OUT Riverside Inn or town of Bracebridge Park on Ecclestone Drive

GENERAL HAZARDS According to Peter Damas at Muskoka Outfitters, kayak buffs run the Sharpe's Creek Cascades when the water levels are extreme. Mortals may consider waiting until levels recede and basking in the primal beauty of the falls while eating a picnic lunch at the bottom. During spring run-off there is considerable flow, and strong current may be difficult and dangerous to paddle against.

ECOLOGY Sharpe's Creek descends from the sandy knolls and old pastureland, overgrown with meadowsweet and poverty grass, east of Highway 11, and then crashes suddenly and dramatically over a series of rock ledges to a deep, clay-based ravine below. Who hasn't driven south on the highway in the early spring to snatch a quick view of this watery sluice and been tantalized by the mystery of where it goes? Within this valley, remnant sedimentation of glacial Lake Algonquin has created a footing for one of Muskoka's richest riparian eco-communities. The diverse communities of vascular plants and the balsam-poplar forest swamp are unusual for Muskoka, particularly over deep clay soils. Two snakes and 17 species of plants here are uncommon in the region.

FEATURES In the early 1800s, Chief William Yellowhead, or Mesquakie, from whom the word Muskoka was derived, had set up his seasonal camp at Kek-kabikong, "at the place of the waterfall," probably because of the superb walleye fishing along the river. The town of Bracebridge, named after Washington Irving's novel *Bracebridge Hall*, was incorporated in 1864. Surprisingly enough, little development has occurred along this scenic route so close to town. Muskoka is certainly reknowned for its beautiful waterfalls. This easy paddling route is highlighted by two prominent fluvial discharges and one rather obscure, almost Tolkien-like cascade. The South Muskoka Canyon is a bedrock fault and ancient glacial spillway. Here, South Falls — probably Muskoka's most illustrated and historic falls — pitches over impervious bedrock to the pool below. The falls can be viewed from the pool below, or from the trail on the south side. Remnants of the old log sluice can be seen along this trail.

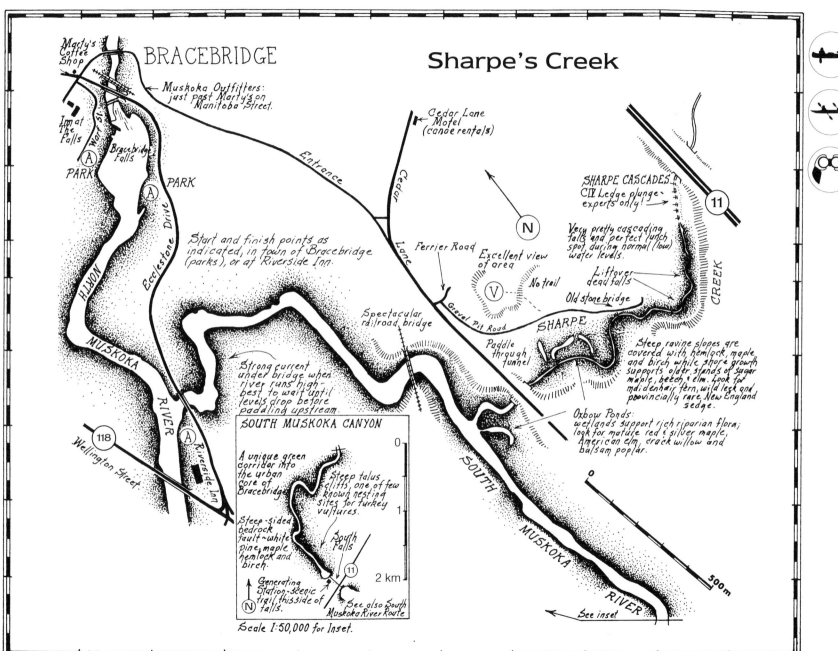

BRACEBRIDGE

Sharpe's Creek

Marty's Coffee Shop

Muskoka Outfitters: just past Marty's on Manitoba Street.

Inn at The Falls

Bracebridge Falls

(A) PARK

(A) PARK

Entrance

Cedar Lane Motel (canoe rental/s)

Cedar Lane

Ferrier Road

(N)

Excellent view of area

(V) No trail

Ecclestone Drive

NORTH

Start and finish points as indicated, in town of Bracebridge (parks), or at Riverside Inn.

SHARPE CASCADES
CIV Ledge plunge - experts only!

Very pretty cascading falls and perfect lunch spot during normal (low) water levels.

Liftover dead falls

Old stone bridge

CREEK

MUSKOKA

RIVER

Spectacular railroad bridge

Gravel Pit Road

SHARPE

Paddle through tunnel

Strong current under bridge when river runs high - best to wait until levels drop before paddling upstream.

Steep ravine slopes are covered with hemlock, maple and birch while shore growth supports older stands of sugar maple, beech & elm. Look for maidenhair fern, wild leek and provincially rare New England sedge.

Oxbow Ponds: wetlands support rich riparian flora; look for mature red & silver maple, American elm, crack willow and balsam poplar.

(118)

Wellington Street

(A)

Riverside Inn

SOUTH MUSKOKA RIVER

0

0

500m

SOUTH MUSKOKA CANYON

A unique green corridor into the urban core of Bracebridge.

Steep talus cliffs, one of few known nesting sites for turkey vultures.

Steep-sided bedrock fault - white pine, maple, hemlock and birch.

South Falls

(11)

2 km

(N)

Generating Station - scenic trail this side of falls.

See also South Muskoka River Route.

Scale 1:50,000 for Inset.

See inset

See also South Muskoka River Route.

(11)

ROSSEAU RIVER
BEAUTY AND THE BEASTS

CLASSIFICATION novice (Crawford's Rapids must be portaged)

DISTANCE 7 km

TIME 2 to 3 hours

SEASON April through October

ELEVATION DROP 133 feet to Lake Rosseau

CAMPSITES none

RAPIDS & FALLS 2 waterfalls, 2 rapids (seasonal running)

PORTAGES 2 (525 m); includes portage around Crawford's Rapids

MAPS Required 31 E/4, 31 E/5

ACCESS Highway 3 (Aspdin Road) bridge, 7 km east of town of Rosseau

TAKE-OUT Rosseau Falls bridge on Rosseau Lake Road 3

ADDITIONAL RESOURCE Audrey Tournay's *Beaver Tales: Audrey Tournay & the Aspen Valley Beavers*

WHITEWATER CHARACTERISTICS & GENERAL HAZARDS
The Rosseau is a rather docile rivulet during the dog days of summer, but in the early season, when the river levels swell, the Rosseau has a high-potency charge. It's a fun ride for avid whitewaterists, but extreme care must be taken when approaching the two falls, normally not a danger during low water, when the take-out point is in relative calm and the current flow is negligible. You can easily check water levels by visiting either of the two falls along the route.

ECOLOGY I love the Rosseau, not just because I live along the middle reaches, but mostly because it is a naturally flowing waterway. It ambles through the hills of Hekla, picking up momentum as it approaches Lake Rosseau, flowing from the northern undeveloped wilderness in quiet abandon, spilling dramatically as it crashes over the granite terraces at the end of its journey. Because of its proximity to the undeveloped north, there is much wildlife activity; deer and moose range through the valley and graze peacefully along the fallow fields; beaver, muskrat, mink and numerous fenland birds can be seen from the canoe. There are remnant pine forests and magnificent white spruce of a beauty unparalleled.

FEATURES Rosseau was the stopping-off place for new settlers travelling to the west; it was also a place of much activity, both commercially and as a tourist mecca. Peter Mutchenbacker operated a sawmill at the mouth of the river, and from 1905 to the early 1930s the mill was run by the Kaufman Furniture Co. The first Muskoka public school was built at Rosseau Falls in 1888.

ASPEN VALLEY WILDLIFE SANCTUARY The wilderness is fast disappearing. As the natural environment becomes fractured and fragmented, further development — and the insecticide-sprayed golf courses and other harmful elements that come with it — put undue stress upon the ecological balance of the land. Audrey Tourney and Tony at the Aspen Valley Wildlife Sanctuary know well the downside to "development," as injured and sick animals are brought by the hundreds to be cared for until they can be released back in to the wild. They now receive animals and birds from distant places, and there are often over a thousand animals wandering the compounds. The Sanctuary is a must-see for those taking an outing on the Rosseau River.

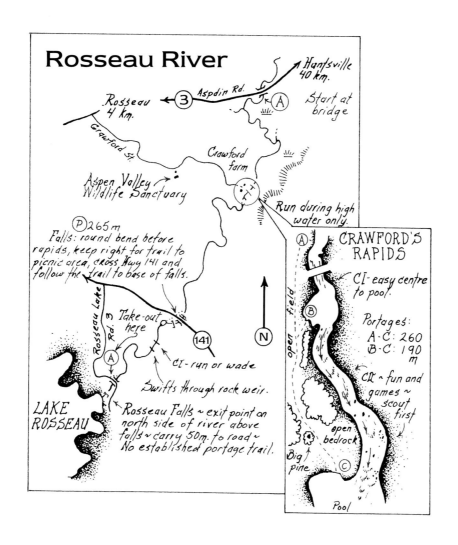

Rosseau River

Huntsville 40 km.

Aspdin Rd.

Rosseau 4 km.

③

Ⓐ Start at bridge

Crawford St.

Crawford farm

Aspen Valley Wildlife Sanctuary

Run during high water only.

Ⓟ 265 m
Falls: round bend before rapids, keep right for trail to picnic area, cross Hwy 141 and follow the trail to base of falls.

Take-out here

Rosseau Lake

Rd. 3

141

CI-run or wade

N

Swifts through rock weir.

Ⓐ

Rosseau Falls ~ exit point on north side of river above falls ~ carry 50m. to road ~ No established portage trail.

LAKE ROSSEAU

CRAWFORD'S RAPIDS

Ⓐ

open field

CI-easy centre to pool.

Ⓑ

Portages:
A·C: 260
B·C: 190 m

CII ~ fun and games ~ scout first

open bedrock

Big pine

Ⓒ

Pool

DEE RIVER
COUNTRY CHARM

CLASSIFICATION novice
DISTANCE 6 km from Three Mile Lake to Windermere
TIME 2.5 to 3 hours
SEASON April through October
ELEVATION DROP 20 m
CAMPSITES none
RAPIDS & FALLS 2 falls, 1 narrow chutes (no runnable whitewater)
PORTAGES 4 (305 m); includes Three Mile Lake portage around Dee Bank Falls
MAP 31 E/4
ACCESS Three Mile Lake Road or Route 21 bridge over the river
TAKE-OUT Windermere Beach
GENERAL HAZARDS Use caution as you approach chutes and falls. Strong prevailing summer winds may impede your final paddle along Lake Rosseau to Windermere.
ECOLOGY The Dee Valley is a glacial till-plain where the clay-based soils are generally deeper and more fertile than most other tillable areas of Muskoka. It's a pastoral setting through farm fields with shorelines of alder, ash and elm. Clark Pond is a magnificent, undeveloped white oak and white pine woodland community, unique in many ways, including as habitat for several rare species of vascular plants. Birds such as the yellow-billed cuckoo and red-shouldered hawk have been sighted but are infrequent visitors. Although turkey vultures are not considered rare, their nest sites are: if you look closely at the talus slope at the north end you may get to see one. The thin soils around the pond and adjacent to the dam make it especially vulnerable to human traffic — please stay in your canoe and walk only on the beaten pathways.
FEATURES Belying its small size, the Dee River once supported bustling communities and five water mills, making it one of the busiest spots in all of Muskoka in the late 1800s. Today it is quiet along the river, and if you look hard enough you'll see some reminders of early commerce tucked under the columbine and sedge along the river banks — old stone ramparts, rusted metal pilings and whispering ghosts.

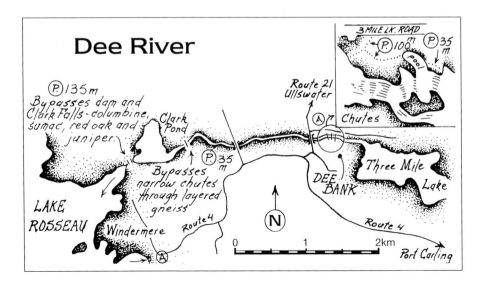

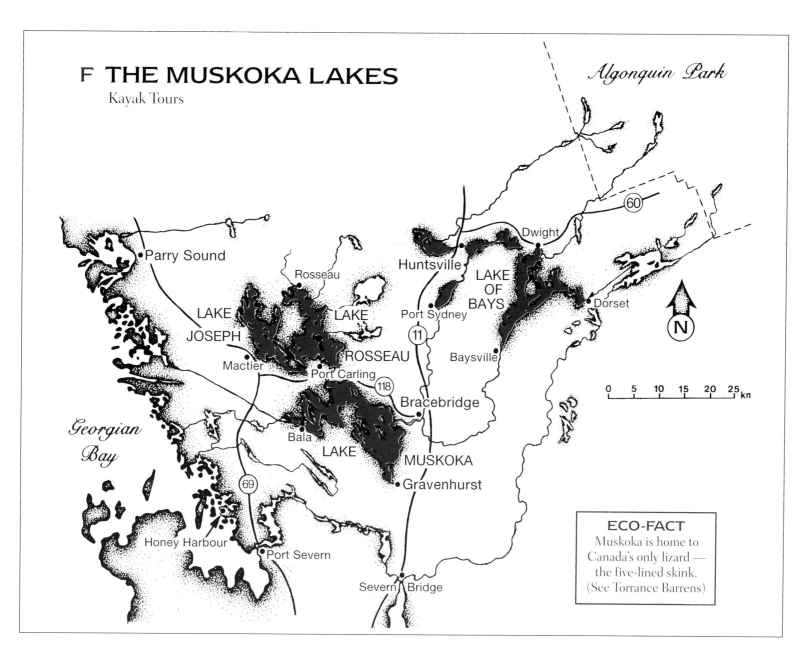

F THE MUSKOKA LAKES
Kayak Tours

Algonquin Park

Parry Sound

Rosseau

Huntsville

Dwight

LAKE OF BAYS

Dorset

N

LAKE JOSEPH

LAKE ROSSEAU

Port Sydney

(11)

Mactier

Port Carling

(118)

Baysville

Bracebridge

(60)

Georgian Bay

Bala

LAKE MUSKOKA

Gravenhurst

0 5 10 15 20 25 km

(69)

Honey Harbour

Port Severn

Severn Bridge

ECO-FACT
Muskoka is home to
Canada's only lizard —
the five-lined skink.
(See Torrance Barrens)

LAKES JOSEPH, ROSSEAU & MUSKOKA
Kayak Tours

These three Muskoka lakes comprise one-third of the lake surface of the Muskoka watershed. The Muskoka Lakes region was settled in the mid-1800s, and the flurry of homesteading and logging reached a peak at the turn of the century. Steamboat transportation gave rise to a growth in tourism and so, as lumbering and farming faltered, business at the luxury hotels in the near wilderness boomed.

Ardent kayakers will find more than enough shoreline to explore, hidden coves and bays where you can enjoy a dip in the buff, and top-notch accommodation and eateries to complete a memorable "soft" adventure vacation. Aside from gawking at the local architecture, which includes Millionaires' Row and 6,000-square-foot boathouses, there are numerous nature-oriented activities one can indulge in. Investigate your options by consulting some of the Muskoka history and tourism literature before you head out.

In the early 1800s, the local First Nations people supposedly referred to Lake Muskoka as "Big Mouth of the River" — Kitshisagan, so called for the place where the Muskoka River drains into the lake from the north. Explorer David Thompson mentioned it in his journals as "Swamp Ground Lake" — Mus ka ko skow oo sak a hagan. Others claim it was named after the Ojibwa chief Mesqua Ukee.

Gain access to Lakes Rosseau and Joseph via Port Carling (Indian River), making a short portage around the locks and climbing a gentle rise of about one meter. The local Natives called Lake Joseph Clear Water because of the clarity and pureness of the water. Lake Rosseau was probably named after fur trader Jean Baptiste Rousseau, while Lake Joseph was named after his father. Lake Rosseau was once the "gateway to the west," where immigrants embarked on the Nipissing Road for destinations in Northern Ontario and Manitoba.

HELPFUL HINTS FOR TRAVELLING
- Carry a cell phone for making reservations or shuttle transfers.
- Carry the appropriate safety gear (flashlight, bilge pump, whistle, tow-lines, paddle float-bag).
- Make advance reservations at inns when possible.
- Take note of prevailing west winds.
- Be wary of motorboat traffic and wake, especially during peak periods, weekends and low-light conditions.
- Respect private property.

SIDE ROUTES Paddle up Muskoka River to Bracebridge, Sharpe's Creek, South Falls and Canyon, down Moon River to the dam, or up the Shadow River.

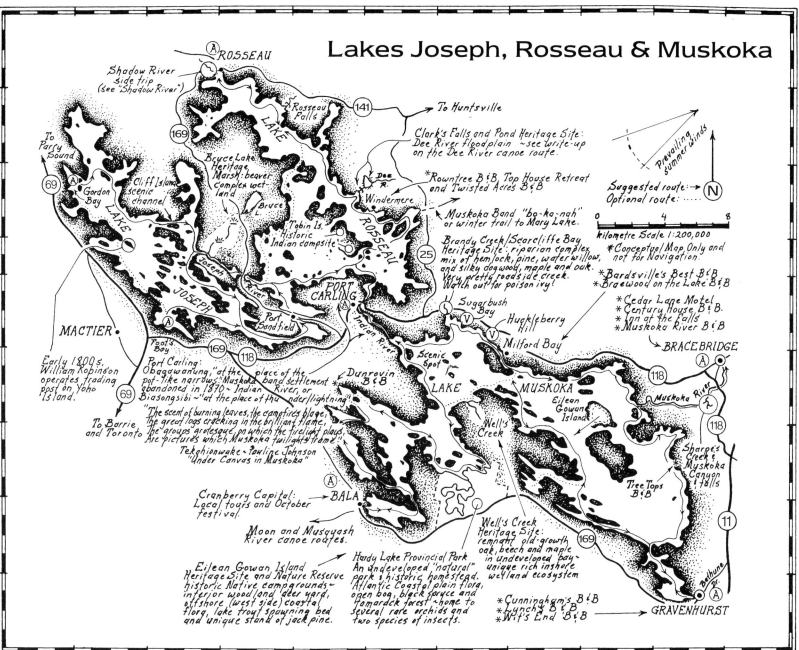

Lakes Joseph, Rosseau & Muskoka

ⒶROSSEAU

Shadow River side trip (see "Shadow River")

Rosseau Falls

141

To Huntsville

169

ROSSEAU LAKE

Bruce Lake Heritage Marsh: beaver complex wetland

Clark's Falls and Pond Heritage Site: Dee River floodplain ~ see write-up on the Dee River canoe route.

Dee R.

Windermere

*Rowntree B&B, Top House Retreat and Twisted Acres B&B

To Parry Sound

69

ⒶGordon Bay

Cliff Island scenic channel

Bruce L.

Muskoka Band "bo-ka-nah" or winter trail to Mary Lake.

25

Brandy Creek/Scarcliffe Bay Heritage Site: riparian complex, mix of hemlock, pine, water willow, and silky dogwood, maple and oak. Very pretty roadside creek. Watch out for poison ivy!

Prevailing summer winds

Suggested route:
Optional route: ....

ⓃN

0   4   8
kilometre Scale 1:200,000

*Conceptual Map Only and not for Navigation.

*Bardsville's Best B&B
*Braewood on the Lake B&B

JOSEPH LAKE

Joseph River

Tobin Is. Historic Indian campsite

PORT CARLING Ⓐ

Sugarbush Bay

Ⓥ

Huckleberry Hill

Ⓥ Milford Bay

*Cedar Lane Motel
*Century House B.B.
*Inn at the Falls
*Muskoka River B&B

→BRACEBRIDGE

Port Sandfield

MACTIER •

Foot's Bay

169

118

Indian River

Scenic Spot

Dunrovin B&B

LAKE   MUSKOKA

Eilean Gowan Island

Ⓐ
118

Muskoka River

118

Early 1800's, William Robinson operates trading post on Yoho Island.

69

Port Carling: Obagawanung, "at the place of the pot-like narrows." Muskoka band settlement abandoned in 1870 ~ Indian River, or Biasongsibi ~ "at the place of thunder/lightning"

"The scent of burning leaves, the campfires blaze, The great logs cracking in the brilliant flame, The groups grotesque, on which the firelight plays, Are pictures which Muskoka twilights frame"

Well's Creek

Sharpe's Creek & Myskoka Canyon & falls

Tree Tops B&B

Tekahionwake ~ Pauline Johnson "Under Canvas in Muskoka"

11

To Barrie and Toronto

Cranberry Capital: Local tours and October festival.

Ⓐ
→BALA

Well's Creek Heritage Site: remnant old-growth oak, beech and maple in undeveloped bay ~ unique rich inshore wetland ecosystem

169

Moon and Musquash River canoe routes.

Eilean Gowan Island Heritage Site and Nature Reserve historic Native campgrounds ~ interior woodland "deer yard," offshore (west side) coastal flora, lake trout spawning bed and unique stand of jack pine.

Hardy Lake Provincial Park An undeveloped "natural" park & historic homestead. Atlantic Coastal plain flora, open bog, black spruce and tamarack forest ~ home to several rare orchids and two species of insects.

Bethune Dr.

Ⓐ

*Cunningham's B&B
*Lynch's B&B
*Wit's End B&B

→GRAVENHURST

LAKE OF BAYS
Kayak Tour

Lake of Bays was once called Nagatoagomen (which, translated, could have meant "white man go home"), but David Thompson claimed that the resident people referred to as the "lake of the forks from its many deep bays and points of land" — Nun ge low e nee goo mark so sak a hagan (say that one fast). The name was shortened to Forked Lake and then Trading Lake and finally to Lake of Bays. Alexander Murray of the Geological Survey of Canada named Mary Lake after his daughter, Fairy Lake because of its beauty, and Peninsula Lake because of its pronounced shape.

This is a gem of a touring route because of the combination and variety of lake and river environments. One of the best start points for this adventure is up on the Big East River near the Dyer Memorial, travelling downriver through the delta to Lake Vernon and Huntsville, and either east to Lake of Bays (via shuttle portage from Peninsula Bay), or south to Mary Lake by way of the Muskoka River. This is an exceptional bed-and-breakfast tour, for a weekend jaunt or a two-week adventure. SIDE ROUTES Up or down the Big East River, through the delta or up to Hoodstown Falls. The Lower Oxtongue River to Marshs Falls is another fascinating environment worth exploring.

Lake of Bays

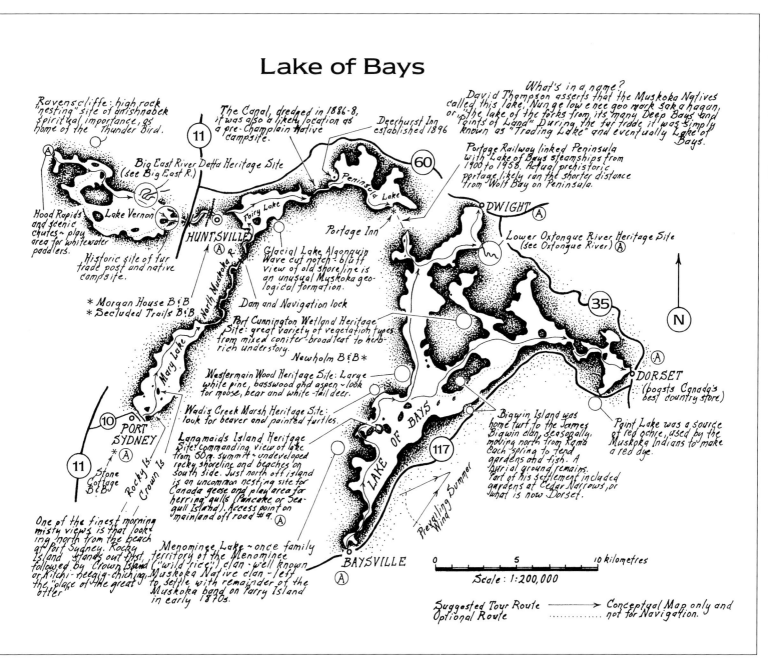

Ravenscliffe: high rock "nesting" site of anishnabek spiritual importance, as home of the "Thunder Bird."

The Canal, dredged in 1886-8, it was also a likely location as a pre-Champlain Native campsite.

Deerhurst Inn established 1896

What's in a name?
David Thompson asserts that the Muskoka Natives called this lake, Nun ge low e nee goo mark sak a hagan, or "the lake of the forks" from its many Deep Bays and Points of Land." During the fur trade it was simply known as "Trading Lake" and eventually Lake of Bays.

Big East River Delta Heritage Site (see Big East R.)

Portage Railway linked Peninsula with Lake of Bays steamships from 1900 to 1958. Actual prehistoric portage likely ran the shorter distance from Wolf Bay on Peninsula.

Peninsula Lake

Fairy Lake

Lake Vernon

Hood Rapids and scenic chutes ~ play area for whitewater paddlers.

HUNTSVILLE

Portage Inn

DWIGHT

Lower Oxtongue River Heritage Site (see Oxtongue River)

Historic site of fur trade post and native campsite.

Glacial Lake Algonquin Wave cut notch - bluff view of old shoreline is an unusual Muskoka geological formation.

North Muskoka R.

* Morgan House B&B
* Secluded Trails B&B

Dam and Navigation lock

Port Cunnington Wetland Heritage Site: great variety of vegetation types from mixed conifer-broadleaf to herb rich understory.

Newholm B&B *

Mary Lake

Westermain Wood Heritage Site: Large white pine, basswood and aspen ~ look for moose, bear and white-tail deer.

Wadis Creek Marsh Heritage Site: look for beaver and painted turtles.

PORT SYDNEY

Langmaids Island Heritage Site: commanding view of lake from 50 m summit ~ undeveloped rocky shoreline and beaches on south side. Just north off island is an uncommon nesting site for Canada geese and play area for herring gulls (Pancake or Seagull Island). Access point on mainland off road #9.

Stone Cottage B&B

Rocky Is.

Crown Is.

DORSET (boasts Canada's best country store)

Bigwin Island was home turf to the James Bigwin clan, seasonally, moving north from Rama each spring to tend gardens and fish. A burial ground remains. Part of his settlement included gardens at Cedar Narrows, or what is now Dorset.

Paint Lake was a source of red ochre, used by the Muskoka Indians to make a red dye.

LAKE OF BAYS

Prevailing Summer Wind

One of the finest morning misty views is that looking north from the beach at Port Sydney. Rocky Island stands out first, followed by Crown Island, or Kitchi-neeqig-chiching, the "place of the great otter."

Menominee Lake ~ once family territory of the Menominee ("wild rice") clan - well known Muskoka Native clan - left to settle with remainder of the Muskoka band on Parry Island in early 1870s.

BAYSVILLE

| 0 | | | 5 | | 10 kilometres |

Scale: 1:200,000

Suggested Tour Route ——→
Optional Route ···········

Conceptual Map only and not for Navigation.

Whitewater Play Zone
MIXING ECOLOGY WITH HYDROLOGY

People of the First Nations had no interest in running rapids. After all, they were paddling rather fragile bark boats and any repairs to canoes would be time consuming. And there was, of course, also the risk of loss of life or limb. The need to manoeuvre unwieldy trade canoes through sections of fast water came from the European, profit-motivated fur industry and the desire to move the product and supplies over long distances within a short period of time. Even then, any serious rapids were bypassed using tracking lines to haul canoes up or down, and gear was usually carried over existing portages. In the early 1900s, during the era of the Canadian canoe brigades, the men sent out as fire-rangers made whitewater paddling part and parcel of a particular, romantic lifestyle; skills were basic and safety equipment was nonexistent. A dump in cold water often meant a long swim and an untimely death on a lonely river. Cedar-canvas canoes were stock items and nothing over a wily Class II was negotiated; boulder gardens were avoided like the plague and it was considered a dishonour if your canoe was ever allowed to touch a rock. Take the bruises, shed a little blood, haul your canoe over the worst, bone-crushing trails, but don't let your canoe kiss a boulder. Repairs were made using tin-can lids pushed between the ribs to support broken planking while Ambroid-impregnated strips of bandana were pasted over rips in the canvas skin. A bad canoeist could be identified easily by the number of repairs made to the hull of his boat.

Today things are quite different, especially with the advent of the "plastic" canoe. At times I get caught up in the adrenaline rush, but I try not to lose sight of the "journey," enjoying more than just the excitement of the whitewater. There's no rule to say that nature can't be enjoyed from a perch in a whitewater canoe. In Muskoka there are plenty of places to practise whitewater savvy in a semi-remote setting. Here are my favourites.

DRIVE-IN SPOTS These are ideal, vehicle-accessible locations where an easy portage alongside the rapids facilitates rerunning.
Oxtongue River Lions Park Rapids, accessible off Highway 60. Depending on water levels, this could be a difficult CIII–CIV with some general playable stuff in between the serious ledges.
Big East River McBrien Rapids, accessible by gravel road north of Billy Bear Lodge. A great CI–CIII run almost anytime of the season.
Gibson River McDonald Chutes, off Highway 69. Early season or highwater play spot with three CII–CIII drops.
North Muskoka River Port Sydney Dam Rapids. Local playspot for kayakers but dependent on water levels (can be dangerous because of chutes below).
South Muskoka River Double-Duty Rapids, Fraserburg Road, south past Purbrook. A CII–CIII "round-the-bend" play spot (respect private property).
Black River Bridge Rapids, town of Vankoungnet. A playful CII.

AFTERNOON JAUNTS These normally require some planning involving shuttles and can be half- to full-day outings starting at an easily accessed departure point.
Musquash River Go Home Lake Dam. A great CIII surfing spot accessible in one hour from Go Home Lake Marina by canoe or kayak.
Hollow River Hollow Falls, off Kawagama Lake Road. A bouldery CII below the falls, or do the whole river for a fabulous day outing.
Oxtongue River Oxtongue Lake to Hunter's Bridge, accessible off Highway 60. An easy CI to CII excursion and preamble to the remainder of the lower run.
Seguin River Mountain Chute. Accessible via Hurdville Road north to the Seguin bridge. CII to CIII dynamo, especially when the water is high.

SERIOUS STUFF Mere mortals should avoid these three places: Sharpe's Falls near Bracebridge, Pretty Channel north off the Severn River, and Hood's Rapids on the Buck River where it empties into Lake Vernon.

CHAPTER THREE

Hiking & Cross-Country Ski Trails

Air, crisp and scented fresh with balsam,
The world sleeps under winter mantle,
Waiting, listening.
Sounds and voices stilled, chilled,
I ski alone, while the trail unfolds before me,
Signature of motion in still wake furled,
Betrays my presence.
Aged pines with corrugated skins,
Elders of the forest beyond reach,
Of meddling industry beseeched,
Defiant, mothering, hovering,
I ski alone.

H. WILSON

HIKING & CROSS-COUNTRY SKI TRAILS

The trail is the stage on which all the drama, the burlesque, the tragedy, and the comedy of the wilderness is played.

GREY OWL

A path through the forest, a well-placed axe blaze on a tree, or a simple cairn of rocks, placed just so, to catch the eye and to let you know that you are, in fact, still on the right track — all are reliable markers of the forgotten wilderness trail.

Today our definition of "trail," like the word "wilderness," has become convoluted to suit opinion that anything of a wild nature should be accessible by any and all means. I do agree that some trails should be so designated as to make access and travel comfortable for the physically challenged, however, the construction of multi-use trails that allow motorized traffic, namely snowmobiles and all-terrain vehicles, in my opinion, does not create what I consider a true trail. I am not a fan of the developed trail, where manmade pathways and superfluous signage spoil the resident charm and drama of the landscape. Of the 43 listed trails in Muskoka, only four offer an honest backcountry experience. All other trails have been developed for general tourism traffic. Experiences vary, however, and some of the developed trails are excellent diversions offering surprisingly eclectic views of Muskoka's physical and ecological environment. In addition, some B & Bs, inns and hotels offer their own brand of trail not listed in this chapter, some presenting exceptional opportunities and privacy not found on public trail systems.

For trail maps and additional information please contact the Muskoka Recreational Trails Council or Muskoka Tourism.

MUSKOKA TRAILS

Ref. No.	Trail Name	Primary Use	Other Uses	Comments
1.	Kahshe Barrens	hiking	skiing	trail is shared with snowmobilers
2.	Hahne Farm	hiking	skiing and snowshoeing	part wood-chip path, some high points
3.	Old Stone Road	hiking	skiing	historical Muskoka road
4.	Devil's Gap	hiking	skiing	natural rock "cleft," part road, snowmobiles
5.	Chamberlain	hiking	skiing	part wood-chip path
6.	Brydon's Bay	hiking	skiing	good view of Lake Muskoka
7.	The Pines Wetland	hiking	skiing	located on Sands Resort property
8.	**KOA**	**skiing**	**hiking and mountain biking**	**featured in detail (see page 128)**
9.	Peterson Wetland	hiking	skiing	located at KOA Nordic Centre
10.	Strawberry Point	hiking	mountain biking	wood-chip trail to lookout
11.	Kerr Park	hiking	skiing and mountain biking	birdwatching around lagoons
12.	**Alport**	**skiing**	**hiking and mountain biking**	**featured in detail (see page 129)**
13.	Bracebridge Bay	walking tour	wheelchair access	pavement along Muskoka River
14.	Covered Bridge	walking tour	mountain biking	part paved road
15.	South Monk	walking tour	mountain biking	part road, used by snowmobilers
16.	Wilson's Falls	walking tour	wheelchair access	spectacular view of falls, joins TC trail
17.	**BRMC**	**skiing, hiking**	**mountain biking**	**featured in detail (see page 127)**
18.	Camp Tawingo	skiing	—	groomed and track set
19.	**Arrowhead Park**	**skiing**	**snowshoeing, hiking**	**featured in detail (see page 132)**
20.	Avery Park	walking tour	mountain biking	located in town of Huntsville
21.	Yonge St. Mountain	mountain biking	walking	packed earth trail, good view
22.	Mary Lake	road cycling	walking	local low-traffic roads
23.	Golf Course	road cycling	walking	local low-traffic roads
24.	Fairy Vista	walking tour	—	paved roads
25.	Grandview	skiing	walking	packed dirt and paved trails
26.	Deerhurst	skiing	walking and mountain biking	50 percent golf course, groomed and track set
27.	Bondi Village	skiing	hiking	groomed and track set trails
28.	**Frost**	**skiing**	**hiking**	**featured in detail (see page 131)**
29.	Port Sydney	road cycling	walking	local low-traffic secondary roads
30.	**Torrance Barrens**	**hiking**	**skiing and star gazing**	**featured in detail (see page 124)**
31.	Artist Loop	walking	biking	mostly road travel
32.	Hazelwood	hiking	skiing	pioneer trail
33.	**Baldwin's**	**skiing**	**hiking**	**featured in detail (see page 130)**
34.	Skeleton Lake	walking	picnicking	old fish hatchery site
35.	Raymond	hiking	skiing and mountain biking	colonization route
36.	Massasauga Park	remote hiking	skiing and winter camping	refer to government map
37.	**Wreck Island**	**hiking**	**—**	**featured in detail (see page 94)**
38.	**McCrae Lake**	**hiking**	**skiing and winter camping**	**featured in detail (see page 126)**
39.	Gibson	hiking	skiing and winter camping	partly detailed in book
40.	Beausoleil Island	hiking	general camping	refer to government map and info
41.	Ganaraska	hiking	skiing	refer to address contact in index
42.	Trans Canada	multi-use	—	part snowmobile and ATV use
43.	Seguin Park to Park	multi-use	—	follows old Booth railway

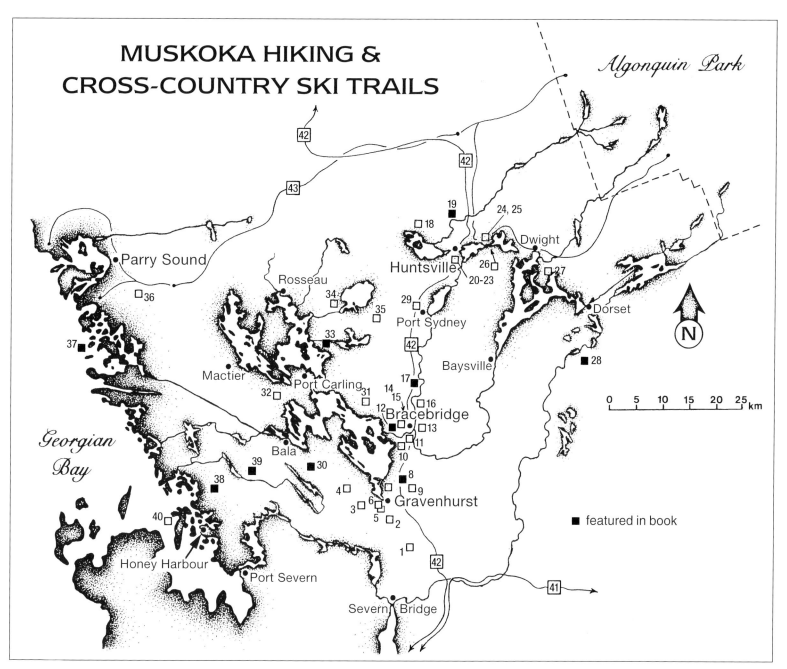

MUSKOKA HIKING & CROSS-COUNTRY SKI TRAILS

Algonquin Park

Parry Sound

Rosseau

42

43

19

18

24, 25

Dwight

Huntsville

26

20-23

36

34

35

29

Port Sydney

27

Dorset

N

33

42

Baysville

28

Mactier

Port Carling

32

31

14

15

17

Bala

Georgian
Bay

39

30

12

16

Bracebridge

13

11

10

8

38

4

7

9

Gravenhurst

40

6

3

5

2

Honey Harbour

1

Port Severn

42

41

Severn Bridge

■ featured in book

0 5 10 15 20 25 km

TORRANCE BARRENS

If it weren't for a handful of dedicated Muskoka stargazers, the Torrance Barrens might never have been designated a "Dark Sky Reserve." Recognized by the Royal Astronomical Society of Canada, the Barrens offer an unrestricted, unblemished view of the heavens. Unusual in its proximity to the GTA (Greater Toronto Area) and other communities in Muskoka, Torrance seems to be perched in just the right spot to evade the invasive light pollution emitted by strip malls, casinos, road lamps and backyard motion lights. The solid 3-billion-year-old granite base is perfect for camera tripod and astronomical instruments too.

The glacially ice-scoured landscape here is more typical of Greenland or the Arctic barrens. Precambrian granite ridges are separated by peat-filled wetlands, and any growth that finds footing in the rock is usually stunted and shaped by the prevailing winds. Highland Pond is surrounded by floating fen-mats, supporting a lush growth of orchids and uncommon flora. Eighteen species of reptiles and amphibians, including Canada's only lizard — the five-lined skink — make their home here. As well, 18 mammals have been documented, including beaver, moose, coyote, flying squirrel (watch out they don't land on your shoulder while you peer through your telescope), grey squirrel, hare, red fox and 28 species of butterflies. Over 90 species of birds have been identified.

One reason Churchill, Manitoba, and Yellowknife in the Northwest Territories have become night-sky destinations is that night-sky viewing is popular with some people of Oriental cultures, who consider a peek at Canada's northern lights beneficial to personal fertility. Now there is the Torrance Barrens. I remember our first walk around the barrens while my wife was nine months pregnant — she gave birth the following day to a little moon-faced boy.

To get there, take Highway 169 to Torrance, turn down Southwood Road (Muskoka Road 13) and drive about 7 km and turn east, over the tracks and watch for signs. There is a small parking area on the left side. Pick up trail maps at the parking lot display. Access by way of Pine Lake is also possible by canoe or kayak from the marina at the east end of the lake.

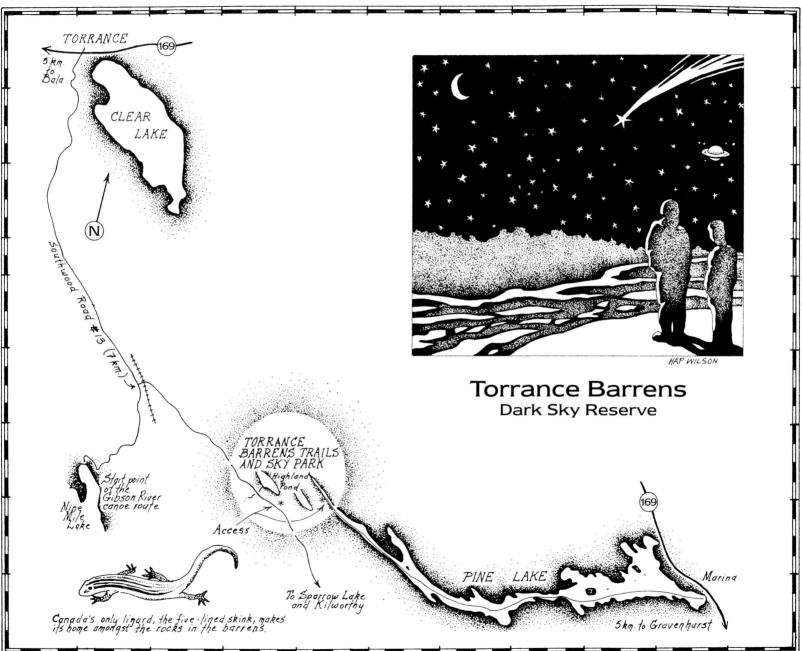

TORRANCE

169

5 km. to Bala

CLEAR LAKE

N

Southwood Road #13 (7 km.)

Nine Mile Lake

Start point of the Gibson River canoe route

TORRANCE BARRENS TRAILS AND SKY PARK

Highland Pond

Access

To Sparrow Lake and Kilworthy

Canada's only lizard, the five-lined skink, makes its home amongst the rocks in the barrens.

PINE LAKE

169

Marina

5 km. to Gravenhurst

HAP WILSON

Torrance Barrens
Dark Sky Reserve

McCRAE LAKE TRAIL

The Five Winds Trail Club out of Toronto started building trails through the Highway 69 corridor about 25 years ago. One trail that stands out from all the others is the McCrae Lake Trail. It starts at the canoe route access point at McDonald Lake and will guide you through some pretty extraordinary Georgian Bay coastal countryside. The trail forms part of a longer system, continuing north past the McCrae outlet to the Gibson River, but for most, the 8-kilometer section from Highway 69 to the viewpoint overlooking the Bay is a good day outing and is easy to follow if you keep an eye on the metal tags and rock cairns. You may decide to pack along an overnight bag. There are campsites at McCrae Lake (south bay), one at a small pond about two-thirds of the way in, and at McCrae Lake (west outlet). McCrae Lake Wilderness Area was first recognized in 1960 for its significant natural importance and scenic beauty. However, in 2001 this 1,943 ha site, under the government's Living Legacy program, was classified as a Conservation Reserve, a move that effectively downgrades its protection status.

Features include the impressive climbing ridge and lookout over McCrae Lake (there is a memorial at the base of the Crow's Nest for a young climber who died there), and bare rock-knolls interspersed with clumps of dense common juniper and stunted red oak. There are tamarack swamps, beaver ponds and the grand-finale view of the Musquash Channel on Georgian Bay with the Giants Tomb Island looming in the distant waters. Because of its undeveloped nature, the McCrae Lake Trail hosts an unchanged biotic community representing the full scope of Georgian Bay coastal communities and a higher than normal number of rare and uncommon species. Allow yourself most of the day for the hike and enough energy to get yourself back to the start point. You'll need lots of time to explore and take pictures along the way, and the walk back is as pleasing as the hike in.

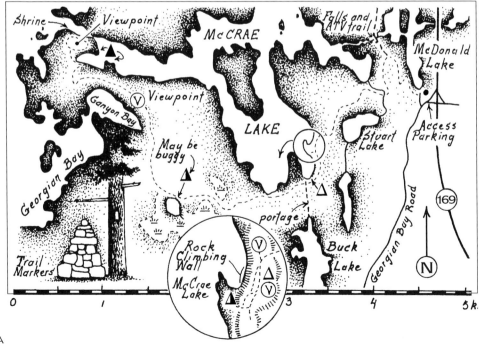

Bracebridge Resource Management Centre (BRMC)

There are four easy trails, 1.5 to 8 km in length, over a natural packed surface. The Muskoka River Trail affords a winter view of Duck Chutes. Trail grooming is somewhat sporadic, and even though signs suggest that skiers leave their dogs at home, locals still disregard the suggestion. It is a great place to haul kids around on a pulk or toboggan. The property was first settled in 1868 by 12 families — Muskoka's first pioneer commune — and was worked up until the 1950s, although little can be seen of their cattle grazing, farming and logging activities today. An impressive mature pine and hemlock forest now makes a perfect habitat for the pine marten and pileated woodpecker. The Ministry of Natural Resources manages the property as a demonstration in resource management techniques; nonetheless, the outstanding attraction of BRMC is the prime white pine stands that have evaded the axe. For more information and conditions, call the OMNR at 705-646-5508.

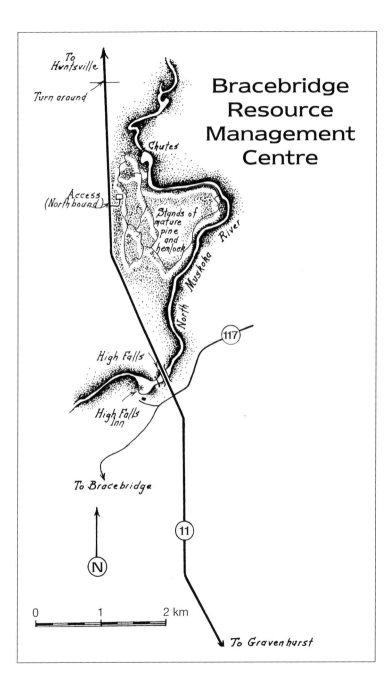

Bracebridge Resource Management Centre

To Huntsville

Turn around

Chutes

Access (Northbound)

Stands of mature pine and hemlock

North Muskoka River

117

High Falls

High Falls Inn

To Bracebridge

11

N

0   1   2 km

To Gravenhurst

KOA NORDIC CENTRE

The central core trail is part of the historic Peterson Road; joined to it are several loops, in all, 17 km of groomed and track-set trails, none of which are very difficult. This is a fully serviced center complete with Adirondack-style warm-up shelter. The outstanding feature of the KOA trails is the diversity of the wetland habitat and surrounding mixed forest — perfect for observing winter wildlife. Contact Paul Cook at 705-687-2333.

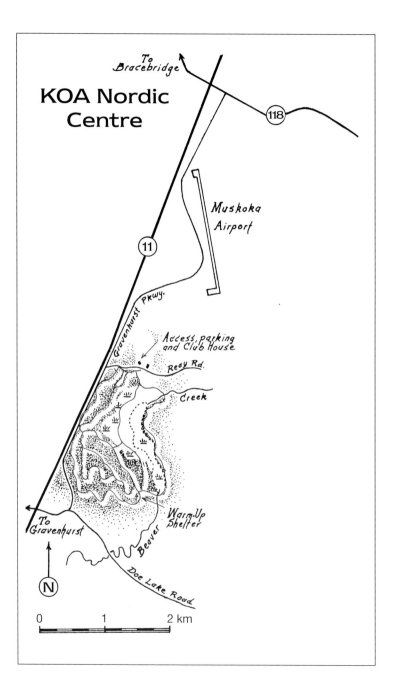

ALPORT TRAILS

These are primarily private trails accessed by permission from Patterson-Kaye Lodge. The groomed base trail, Jack Rabbit Loop, is 2.7 km in length, and it doubles as a hiking trail in summer. Linked to this trail are about 12 km of "backcountry" user-groomed trails, best hit after a fresh fall of snow. Terrain varies from challenging center core to pastoral farm fringe along the east boundary. Every species of wintering bird can be found here, from nuthatch to pileated woodpecker, and there are frequent sightings of deer, ruffed grouse and snowshoe hare. There is a steep trail connecting the Santa's Village parking lot but it is generally icy and dangerous on the downslope. For information call Patterson-Kaye Lodge at 1-800-561-6998 or e-mail pklodge@muskoka.com.

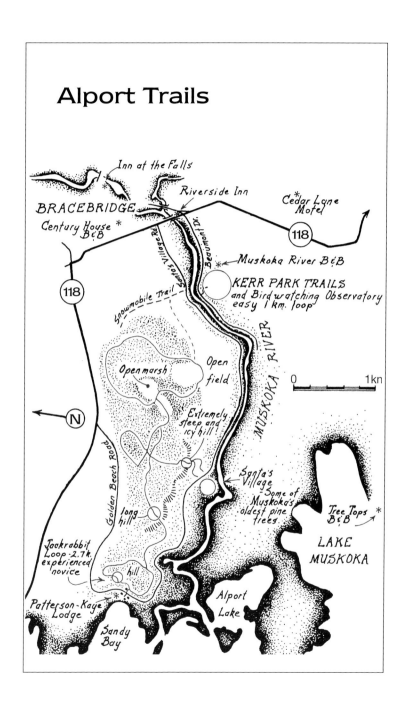

BALDWIN'S RESORT TRAILS

This quintessential Muskoka lodge offers one of the best ski trail networks in central Ontario. Meticulous care and pride go into every detail here, from trail placement to grooming. These are "private" trails for guests of Baldwin's Lodge or registered guests of the listed Windermere B & Bs. Over 20 km of trails are split between open golf-course flats and hardwood forest hills. Trails are professionally groomed and track set and range in difficulty from very easy to very challenging. The only thing you have to watch out for here is running into a deer on the "highland fling." For bookings call Baldwin's Lodge at 1-800-461-1728.

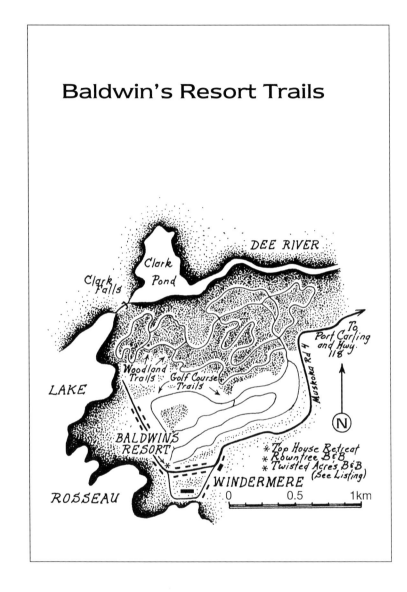

Baldwin's Resort Trails

FROST CENTRE NORDIC TRAILS

Cross-country skiing doesn't get any better than this. There are 25 km of groomed trails managed by the Ski Friends of the Frost Centre. Set amid the Haliburton Highlands on the Muskoka fringe, the trails run through extraordinary Canadian Shield topography. You'll enjoy rugged backcountry terrain, the majesty of the pine forest, giant hemlocks, cliff lookouts, frozen waterfalls and optimum opportunities for wildlife viewing. Two warm-up shelters are well placed for longer treks and for those out winter camping. Donations are accepted for trail maintenance, and trail fee or seasonal pass is required. Contact the SFFC, c/o Frost Centre, R.R. 2 Minden, Ontario, K0M 2K0, or at 705-766-9677.

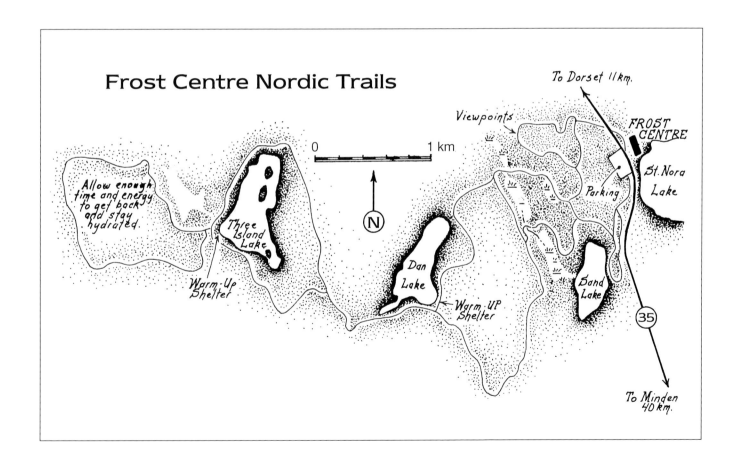

ARROWHEAD PROVINCIAL PARK NORDIC TRAILS

According to Mike Derbyshire, Arrowhead's ski technician, traffic on the Nordic trails is up in recent years, attracting a higher caliber of skier. Arrowhead is a full-service facility and the trails are professionally groomed and track set, offering 27 km of novice to expert runs for both traditional and skate skier. There is also a 3 km snowshoe trail to a nearby waterfall. There is a fee for trail use. For updated trail conditions and events call 705-789-9711.

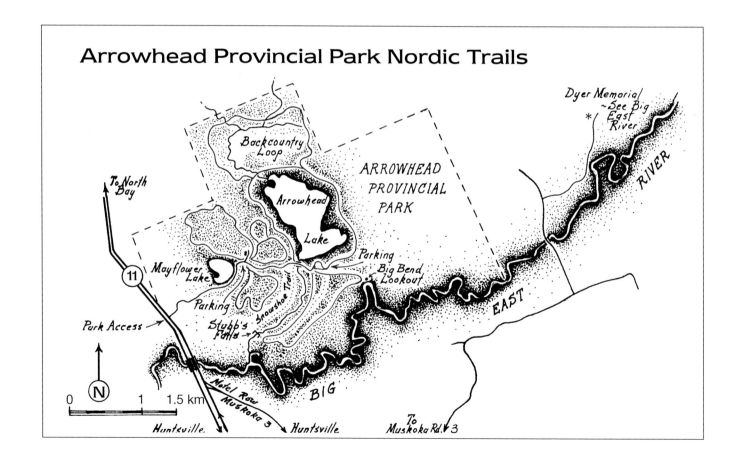

Muskoka's Old-Growth Pine Forest

On first coming to this country nothing surprised me more than the total absence of trees about the dwelling houses and cleared lands, the axe of the chopper relentlessly levels all before him. Man appears to contend with the trees of the forest as though they were his most obnoxious enemies; for he spares neither the young sapling in its greenness, nor the ancient trunk in its lofty pride; he wages war against the forest with fire and steel.

C. P. TRAILL, 1833, *THE BACKWOODS OF CANADA*

The Muskoka pine never stood much of a chance. Pioneer homesteaders burned it to clear the land; timber companies cut it down and floated it to the mills by the millions of cubic feet, and by the late 1800s there wasn't much left of the lofty pine except stumps and slash.

"The entire area has been logged and burned over since the late 1700s," claims district MNR forester Dave Deugo. He's mostly right about that. When I broached the subject of "old-growth" pine, he winced. "There is none," he told me smartly. But old-guard foresters are a hard lot to change.

Muskoka does indeed have several areas of old-growth pine. Unlike the trees in Temagami to the north — the limit of the great pine forests where blockades and environmental sleuthing forced the government into recognizing old-growth forests in this province — Muskoka trees grow faster because of climate and soil conditions. And because of the type of forestry practised 150 years ago (horse drawn and river driven), the impact on the landscape itself was minimal (as opposed to clear-cutting, scarifying, road building and slash burning used today). There are several remnant pine forests coming of age — the more reason to protect it — and here is where to find them:

Dividing Lake Nature Reserve Recently expanded through the government's Living Legacy program, Dividing Lake claims south-central Ontario's largest remaining old-growth pine stand. See the Hollow River route description for more information.

Cardwell Township Conservation Reserve Newly designated, this 996 ha prime forest, surrounded by the historic Nipissing and Bear Cave Road, boasts of trees exceeding 100 years of age. There is no designated access to the forest, but plans are in the works for a hike-only old-growth trail.

Massasauga Provincial Park There are two locations of note inside the park: one between Spider and Vicary Lakes, and the other on the south side of Mathews Island.

Curtain to Moon Falls One of the prettiest corridors in all of Muskoka, with pine to boot! This is what Muskoka used to look like.

Black River I found several small blocks of old-growth along the river with breast-height diameter (bhd) wider than the length of my paddle. Best site is just above Highway 118 along the meanders, and you can reach it by canoe or by a short bushwhack off the Black River Road.

Really accessible places There are several small, scattered stands and one fairly large one near the parking lot at BRMC (Bracebridge Resource Management Centre) and along the trail to the subdivision near the Woodchester Villa in Bracebridge.

By no means is this the extent of it; there are pockets and shorelines rich with old pine to enjoy — the Muskoka rivers, Musquash River, the Big East. It's out there. But when you think that there were once 300 to 400 of these huge trees growing per acre, there really isn't much left.

CHAPTER FOUR

End Notes

And up on the hills against the sky,
A fir tree rocking its lullaby,
Swings, swings.
Its emerald wings,
Swelling the song that my paddle sings.

PAULINE JOHNSON, TEKAHIONWAKE (1861–1913),
FROM HER POEM "THE SONG MY PADDLE SINGS"

CAMPFIRE MUSE

I spent the summer traveling, I got half way across my backyard.

NATURALIST LOUIS AGASSIZ

As the evening wanes, I stoke the embers of the fire and throw on another log. Nighthawks circle about in the warm autumn thermals, above the ghost mist, and swoop in arcs over the lake beyond my campsite. A loon cruises by, inspecting the overturned canoe at the water's edge. I sit back against a log, sip my coffee and begin writing in my journal…

"This place called Muskoka, with all its patent ghosts, its histories, its landscapes…in no insignificant capacity, has stirred my soul and worked its magic convincingly, thoroughly and pleasantly. Having been fooled by its seemingly ostentatious character, believing that one could not possibly find solace here, away from the convening summer crowds, I now reform that opinion and stand on a more enlightened ground. I can honestly convey my surprise and elation at what I found, on these rivers, over these rocky vales, through these primitive fenlands. For whatever reasons we seek out quiet places, regardless of how we define that lucid stillness or the self-fulfillment of adventure, it can be found here."

But despite all this, there remains a looming threat of change. The exhilaration of the experience, for me, also carries with it a lamentable truth. Our environment is constantly being compromised and challenged by our meddling. Muskoka has, over the years, allowed and even encouraged its share of ill-conceived development. But a lack of consideration for the natural world can only mar Muskoka's reputation as a place to get away from it all. Environmental awareness shouldn't be an event or a blue box, but a process and an ongoing consciousness, requiring constant vigilance.

I light my pipe. It is dark outside of the fire glow and the night chill drifts in. I move closer to the fire. I think about the places I've been over the past four years. To be blessed by such adventure in my life, to feel the breath of the land and to meet the ghosts who now sit with me around the campfire is nothing short of remarkable. An epiphany. We all share a drag on the pipe. The smoke drifts lazily upward and gets lost within the outstretched arms of the old pine.

Bed & Breakfast Listing

This is not a complete listing; it includes only those establishments that answered a general ecotourism questionnaire indicating a special interest in offering eco-travel and special services. For a complete listing, visit the B & B website at **www.bbmuskoka.com**. Your hosts are knowledgeable about where to go in Muskoka and will be more than happy to help you plan a memorable excursion. The activities listed are an abbreviated compilation provided by the B & B operator.

"Inn to Inn" adventures can be arranged by contacting the association or any establishment listed below.

Algonquin Getaway Your host is Jamie Honderich at **705-789-1727** (*morganbb@vianet.on.ca*). Open year-round with room for 6 guests. Extended stay-over is possible with equipment rentals nearby. Shuttles can be arranged. Breakfast only. Activities include fishing and canoeing on the Oxtongue River.

Bardsville's Best Your hosts are Don and Carol Goltz at **705-764-1262**. Open year-round with 5 beds. Extended stay-over is possible but no equipment rentals on site, although shuttles may be arranged. Additional meals are possible with a full range of activities available close by.

Braewood on the Lake Your hosts are Mike and Michelle Braden at **705-764-1125** (*braewood@muskoka.com*). This is a full season facility with 4 beds. Extended stay-over is possible but no equipment rentals or shuttle service. Bag lunches can be arranged for a variety of nearby activities.

Century House Your host is Sandy Yudin at **705-645-9903** (*cnturybb@muskoka.com*). Open year-round with 4 beds. This facility will arrange extended visits. Equipment is available nearby and one-person shuttles can be booked on site. Bag lunches can be supplied for hiking, canoeing, cycling and skiing excursions.

Cunningham's Your hosts are Leona and Dave Cunningham at **705-687-4511**. This B & B has 4 beds and is open all year with extended stay-over possible by arrangement. No equipment rentals on site or shuttle service. Only breakfast is served, so hikers trekking the nearby trails will have to pack additional meals.

Dunrovin Your hosts are Wilsie and Bob Mann at **705-765-7317** (*dunrovin@muskoka.com*). Extended visits can be arranged at this lakeside B & B with 5 beds. Limited equipment available on site; shuttles will be arranged upon request. Additional meals can be supplied, and activities include canoeing, kayaking, skiing and hiking.

Inn at the Falls Year-round services with 42 rooms. Resident ghosts Bob, Charlie and Sarah live in the kitchen, Room 105 and the dining room. (If a dog with a halo above it appears at the end of your bed, don't be too surprised.) Built in 1876, this attractive inn can be reached at **705-645-2245** (*iatf@muskoka.com*). Stay as long as you want and pick up rental gear nearby (no shuttle service). Full-service dining room and pub with numerous activities close by.

Kruger's Your hosts are Bruce and Lynn Kruger at **705-645-5814** (*kruger@muskoka.com*). This four-season facility with 5 beds does not have rental equipment or shuttles but will supply bag lunches for day canoeing or kayaking outings.

Lynch's Your host is Jim Lynch at **705-687-2048** (*lynch@muskoka.com*). This is a year-round business with 3 beds, and extended stay-over can be arranged. There is one canoe on the premises for use by guests but no shuttle service or meals other than breakfast. There are hiking trails nearby.

Morgan House Your hosts are Pam Carnochan and Jamie Honderich at **705-789-1727** (*morganbb@vianet.on.ca*). Operating year-round, this 4-bed B & B can arrange extended visits, and equipment rentals. There is no shuttle service. Activities include hiking, biking, skiing and nature photography.

Portage Inn Your host is Theresa at **705-788-7171** (*portage@muskoka.com*). This full-season B & B has 9 beds with the option to stay as long as you wish. Canoes, kayaks and bicycles are available for guests but no shuttle service is available. Additional meals can be arranged and activities include canoeing and kayaking excursions.

Rowntree Cottage Your hosts are Gid and Ruth Rowntree at 705-769-3640 (*rowntree.home@sympatico.ca*). Open from June to October. They can provide 7 beds, extended visits and have one canoe for use by guests. Additional rental equipment and shuttle service is not provided. Primary activities are canoeing and kayaking.

Secluded Trails Your hosts are Judy and Hugh Parker at **705-789-8008** (*secluded@secludedtrails.com*). There are 6 beds available at this year-round B & B. Extended stay-over is an option but you will have to bring your own equipment; the canoe and shuttle is available to move luggage only. Bag lunches can be arranged for nature walks and ski treks. Stargazing is one of their hallmark activities.

Severn River Inn Your host is Kaaren Brandt at **705-689-6333** (*sri@severnriverinn.com*). This historic inn offers 9 rooms and resident ghosts and has a full-service dining room and pub. Extended visits are possible and equipment rentals are available close by but there is no on-site shuttle service. Activities include hiking, canoeing and kayaking along the Severn River.

Stone Cottage Your hosts are Joanne and Bill Chalmers at **705-385-3547**. Extended stay-overs can be arranged at this 3-bed, year-round B & B. Equipment rentals are close by, but no shuttle service or additional meals are available. Primary activities include canoeing and nature trail hikes.

Top House Retreat Hosts are Don and Barbara Dutton at **705-769-3338** (*tophouse@muskoka.com*). This is a four-season facility with 4 beds and an option to lengthen your visit. No on-site equipment but shuttles can be arranged and bag lunches supplied for skiing and nature trail hikes.

Tree Tops Hosts are Merle and Ron Bezoff at **705-645-6271**. Tree Tops operates from may to November, offers 3 beds and can arrange for any length of stay-over. Equipment can be rented nearby but there is no shuttle service on site. Additional meals can be arranged and primary activities are canoeing and kayaking excursions on Lake Muskoka.

Twisted Acres Your hosts are Marlene and Bill Webb at **705-769-3003** (*tabandb@vianet.on.ca*). Extended stay-over is possible in their efficiency units. This is a year-round business with 6 beds, nearby outfitting, on-site shuttle service and complete meal package. On site activities include nature hikes and skiing with canoeing and kayaking possible nearby.

Wit's End Your host is Carol Wagg at **705-687-6992** (*info@witsendbb.com*). Year-round services, 3 beds, extended stay-over option and nearby equipment rentals. Shuttle service and additional meals can be arranged upon request. Hiking trails and canoeing are the primary activities.

Wolf Den Bunkhouse Your host is Jamie Honderich at **705-789-1727** (*morganbb@vianet.on.ca*). This backpacker hostel is open from May to October and sleeps 44 people in bunkhouses and private cabins. Extended stay-over can be arranged as well as outfitting services and shuttles to nearby trails, water routes and attractions. The Bunkhouse has a fully equipped kitchen. It is also available for group rental in the winter months.

Muskoka Outfitters

Algonquin Outfitters — Huntsville/Oxtongue Lake
R. R. 1 Dwight, ON P0A 1H0, 705-635-2243
canoe@muskoka.com

Call of the Wild — Huntsville
23 Edward Street, Markham, ON M3P 2L9, 905-471-9453
adventures@callofthewild.ca

Georgian Bay Islands National Park — Georgian Bay
Box 28, Honey Harbour, ON P0E 1E0, 705-756-2415
info@gbi.pch.gc.ca

Eco Explorations — Huntsville
Box 5559, Huntsville, ON P1H 2L5
www.eco-explorations.com
explore@eco-explorations.com

Muskoka Outfitters — Bracebridge
60 Manitoba Street, Bracebridge, ON P1L 1S1, 705-646-0492
www.muskokaoutfitters.com
mail@muskokaoutfitters.com

Muskoka Adventure — Gravenhurst
1060 Muskoka Road S., Gravenhurst, ON P1P 1K6
www.muskokaadventure.com
oakwoodmotel@muskokaadventure.com

Northern Edge — Algonquin/Huntsville
General Delivery, South River, ON P0A 1X0
Winter address: 375 Bartlet Drive, Windsor, ON N9G 1V1
www.algonquincanada.com

Portage Store — Algonquin/Huntsville
Box 10009, Algonquin Park, ON P1H 2H4, 705-633-5622
portage@inforamp.net

Up North Outfitters — Georgian Bay
Geoff & Teresa Greasley, Delawana Inn Resort
42 Delawana Drive, Honey Harbour, ON P0E 1E0, 705-756-0204

Swift Canoe & Kayak — Gravenhurst/Georgian Bay
Highway 11 South, Gravenhurst, ON P1P 1R1, 705-687-3710
swift@swiftcanoe.com

Windsong Adventures — Huntsville
705-635-1537
www.windsongadventures.com
canoenorth@sympatico.ca

White Squall Paddling Centre
53 East Carling Bay Road, Nobel, ON P0G 1G0,
705-342-5324, fax 705-342-1975
www.whitesquall.com
info@whitesquall.com
or 19 James Street, Parry Sound, ON P2A 1T4, 705-746-4936

Eskakwa Wilderness Adventures
Box 288, Rosseau, ON P0C 1J0, 705-732-8254,
fax 705-732-8255
www.canadawilderness.com/eskakwa
eskakwa@vianet.on.ca

FOR MORE INFORMATION

Muskoka Recreational Trails Council
Box 360, Bracebridge, Ontario, P1L 1R6
705-645-6840

Trans Canada Trail Foundation
6104 Sherbrooke St. West, Montreal, Quebec H4A 1Y3
E-mail info@tctrail.ca

Park to Park Trail
C/o Parry Sound Area Community Business and Development
17 Bay St., Unit C, Parry Sound, Ontario P2A 1S4
E-mail info@parktoparktrail.com

Seguin Trail
Ministry of Natural Resources
Parry Sound District
7 Bay St., Parry Sound, Ontario P2A 1S4
705-746-4201

Natural Resources Information Centre
300 Water St., P.O. Box 7000, Peterborough, Ontario K9J 8M5
General Inquiries 1-800-667-1940

Small Craft Guide to Trent-Severn Waterway, 1989, 7th edition
Small Craft Guide to Georgian Bay, 1988, 3rd edition
Department of Fisheries and Oceans Publication

SUGGESTED READING

There are too many good Muskoka books to mention here. Check your local library or bookstores for more information.

Callan, Kevin. *A Paddler's Guide to Ontario's Cottage Country*. Erin: Boston Mills Press, 2003. Expanded and revised, first published in 1993 as *Cottage Country Canoe Routes*.

Callan, Kevin. *A Paddler's Guide to the Rivers of Ontario and Quebec*. Erin: Boston Mills Press, 2003. First published in 1999 as *Further Up the Creek*.

Chrismar. *The Adventure Map — Poker Lake & Moon River Routes*. Uxbridge: 2000.

Craik, Anne. *Country Walks*. Erin: Boston Mills Press, second edition, 2000.

Finlay, Tom. *Muskoka Book of Lists*. Toronto: Venture Press, 1982.

Long, Gary. *This River the Muskoka*. Erin: Boston Mills Press, 1989.

Mussio Ventures Ltd. *Backroad Mapbook — Algonquin Region*. New Westminster, B.C.: 1999.

Pryke, Susan. *Explore Muskoka*. Erin: Boston Mills Press, revised edition, 2000.

Reynolds, Jonathan & Heather Smith. *Kayaking Georgian Bay*. Erin: Boston Mills Press, 1999. www.chrismar.com

BIBLIOGRAPHY

Chambers, Legasy & Bentley. *Forest Plants of Central Ontario*. Edmonton: Lone Pine, 1996.

Ministry of Natural Resources. *Ontario's Living Legacy — Land Use Strategy*. Government of Ontario, 1999.

Long, Gary. *This River the Muskoka*. Erin: Boston Mills Press, 1989.

Reid, Ron & Bonnie Bergsma. *Natural Heritage Evaluation of Muskoka*. Vancouver: Douglas & McIntyre, 1994.

ACKNOWLEDGMENTS

There are many individuals, sponsors and associations who must be recognized for their contributions to and support of this project. From the financial assistance for the research to offering a hot cup of coffee on a cold, drizzly spring day, there are just too many people to list here. You are all etched in my mind and heart and I thank each and every one of you for lending your support.

To the people who got the bureaucratic ball rolling, to individual sponsors, friends and family who contributed positive energy, those who shared their field notes, favorite routes, contacts and local information, to my tripping friends, and to those who were always there to lend a hand — my sincere gratitude. Thanks to Martha Armstrong, Gillian and Peter Aykroyd, the Bracebridge Public Library, Roger Bragg, Penny and Bob Britnell, John Campbell, Carl and Rebecca Campetelli, Murray Clarke, Randy Clark, Elene Freer, Bob Hunter and Stephen Hurlbut (CITY TV), Bob and Wilsie Mann (B & B Association), Marty and Dana (Marty's Coffee House), Chris Milner, John and Pam Newton, Kim Northmore, Mayor Scott Northmore, Mark Patterson, Rudy, Ron Reid, Al and Deloris Skilliter, and Lynn and Peter Taylor.

I'd also like to thank Wade and Aviva Hemsworth for driving me to the Huntsville hospital after my near brush with death on Highway 60 (the embarrassing face-plant after being tossed off my bicycle when the front brake jammed). Next time I will wear my helmet! Kudos to Anne and Gault McTaggart for picking up my canoe and what was left of my bike, and for taking care of Steph and the kids.

Thanks also to my publisher and editor at Boston Mills Press for having faith.

And most important, I would like to thank my dearest friend, confidante and wife, Stephanie, for her patience and loving support through it all, and for bringing into this world two beautiful Muskoka-born children.

FINANCIAL CONTRIBUTORS

Ontario Ministry of Agriculture, Food and Rural Affairs
Algonquin Outfitters
BDO Ward Associates
Town of Bracebridge
Town of Gravenhurst
Town of Huntsville
Township of Georgian Bay
Muskoka Outfitters
Muskoka Tourism Marketing Agency
Up North Outfitters

EQUIPMENT SPONSORS

Johnson Outdoors Canada
Swift Canoe & Kayak
Muskoka Outfitters
Knudsen Canoe Pack
Bracebridge Public Library Archives

OTHER MUSKOKA BOOKS FROM BOSTON MILLS PRESS

At the Water's Edge: Muskoka's Boathouses John de Visser & Judy Ross
1-55046-082-X

A Paddler's Guide to Ontario's Cottage Country Kevin Callan
1-55046-383-7

Beaver Tales Audrey Tournay and the Aspen Valley Beavers
1-55046-410-8

The Boatbuilders of Muskoka A.H. Duke & William Gray
1-55046-074-9

By Steam Boat & Steam Train: The Huntsville & Lake of Bays Railway and Navigation Companies Niall MacKay 0-919822-738

Daytripper 4: 50 Trips in Cottage Country Donna Carpenter
1-55046-161-3

Ditchburn Boats: A Muskoka Legacy Harold Shield & Bev McMullen
1-55046-412-4

Explore Muskoka Susan Pryke & G. W. Campbell 1-55046-241-5

The Greatest Little Motor Boat Afloat Dodington, Fossey, Gockel, Ogilvie & Smith 0-919783-899

Guide Book & Atlas of Muskoka and Parry Sound Districts 1879 John Rogers 1-55046-307-1

The History of Clevelands House: Magic Summers Susan Pryke
1-55046-343-8

Micklethwaite's Muskoka John Denison 1-55046-069-2

Muskoka John de Visser & Judy Ross 1-55046-004-8

Muskoka Souvenir John de Visser & Judy Ross 1-55046-125-7

Muskoka II John de Visser & Judy Ross 1-55046-237-7

Shelter at the Shore: The Boathouses of Muskoka John de Visser & Judy Ross 1-55046-345-4

Steamboat Era in the Muskokas Richard Tatley *Vol I: To the Golden Years* 0-919822-509 *Vol II: Golden Years to Today* 0-919783-104

Summer Cottages John de Visser & Judy Ross 0-7737-2553-9

Windermere Richard Tatley 1-55046-235-0

Windermere House: The Tradition Continues Susan Pryke
1-55046-288-1

Wood & Glory: Muskoka's Classic Launches William Gray & Timothy Du Vernet 1-55046-177-X

Yoga in a Muskoka Chair Susan Feathers & Carol Sherman
1-55046-368-3

www.bostonmillspress.com

CANOEING AND HIKING
WILD MUSKOKA

Midway 'twixt earth and heaven,
A bubble in the pearly air I seem
To float upon the sapphire floor, a dream
Of clouds of snow,
Above, below
Drift with my drifting, dim and slow,
As twilight drifts to even.

PAULINE JOHNSON, TEKAHIONWAKE (1861–1913),
FROM HER POEM "SHADOW RIVER: MUSKOKA"

For Alexa Skye, born west of the East
and east of the Moon.